# Out of a Dead End
# Into the Unknown

# Out of a Dead End Into the Unknown

## Notes on Gorbachev's Perestroika

Vladimir K. Yegorov

Translated by David Floyd

**e** edition q, inc.
Chicago, Berlin, London, Tokyo, and Moscow

The original German edition was published under the title, *Aus der Sackgasse in die Ungewissheit: Die Perestroika des Michail Gorbatschow,* by edition q Verlags-GmbH, Berlin.

Original English-language paperback edition
©1993 by edition q, inc., Carol Stream, Illinois.

Library of Congress Cataloging-In-Publication Data

Yegorov, Vladimir K.
   [Aus der Sackgasse in die Ungewissheit. English]
   Out of a dead end : notes on Gorbachev's perestroika / Vladimir K. Yegorov : translated by David Floyd.
      p. cm.
   Includes bibliographical references.
   ISBN 0-86715-267-2
   1. Soviet Union—Politics and government—1985–1991.
2. Perestroika. 3. Gorbachev, Mikhail Sergeyevich, 1931–
I. Title.
DK288.E3413   1993                                         93-24701
320.947—dc20                                                    CIP

All rights reserved. This book or any part thereof may not be reproduced, stored in a retrieval system, or transmitted in any form or by any means, electronic, mechanical, photocopying, recording, or otherwise, without prior written permission of the publisher.

Edited by Carl Wilson
Jacket design by Royce Becker
Manufactured in the United States of America

# Contents

Preface VII
Introduction XI
1 Designs in the Arras 1
2 Was Perestroika Really Necessary? 17
3 Why Gorbachev? 27
4 The Philosophy of Renewal 39
5 Gorbachev and Public History 51
6 Evolution, Revolutionary Evolution, Revolution 65
7 What Happened in the Perestroika Years? 81
8 Gorbachev's Algorithm 119
Conclusion 145
Notes 149

# Preface

A year has passed since the end of the historical period to which this book is dedicated. And just as a year ago, I leaf through the pages and wonder whether I have been accurate and objective in my observations and correct in my conclusions.

Frankly speaking, I would now emphasize some things differently. I would characterize more precisely the politicians of Perestroika, including its leader. A year in current history is quite a short time. As the poet said, "When you are close, face to face, you cannot see a face." But as for the main issues, I basically remain with the same positions I held before.

The year 1992 cast the central theme of this book into even greater relief. When Gorbachev began Perestroika, he brought the country out of a dead end. There could have been no other way. That was clear. But more often than not, he did not know where he was taking the country. It turns out it was into the unknown. All of Gorbachev's statements since he has become a "pensioner" confirm this—even when he claims the opposite. The development of Russia and the other republics of the former USSR also bear this out. Gorbachev never imagined the events that would occur today, neither those which instill hope, even in our most difficult time, nor those which are tragic.

This last year has also proved (unfortunately) that the division of the USSR along the illogical borders of the republics aggravates the mistakes of the Bolsheviks. Now these blunders have only been compounded. It was absurd in the first place to mark these boundaries even if they were permeable. It is even more absurd to fix them as firm state borders. And the neo-Bolshevik nature of power in a number of the former USSR republics only worsens the problem.

Time has also shown that the Russian people and Gorbachev evaluated the history of the country and socialism in different ways. Now the former number one communist and president says that not only is he no longer a communist, he is not a socialist either. At least he no longer believes in socialism. Even so, it does not follow that his policies reflected this, although references can be heard in his speeches to the continuing realization in Russia of the profound designs of Perestroika. In his last years in power, he no longer determined the fundamental orientation of the country. He no longer shaped the course of events but played catch-up, always arriving too late. He was also delayed with his own personal, political, and ideological Perestroika. After all, the retreat from socialism is a stage that millions of my fellow citizens have already passed. So he did not win any new friends on that score, but lost quite a few old ones.

My country is going through a difficult time. Economic reform is going worse than even the skeptics imagined. The opposition is threatening a backlash. The forces grouping around power forebode the possibility of a return to the old. Everyone has their own interests. But the country and the people cannot be pushed backwards. Perestroika and the post-Perestroika year have once again proved that Russia needs leaders with a firm political will. Not leaders who promise, but leaders who do. We have not been so fortunate to have those kind of leaders in the past, and we do not have them even now. Our hope today is in the younger people who were, in fact, awakened by Perestroika, regardless of our attitude toward it.

Perestroika did not turn out the way it was planned, but it was not in vain. That, I think, is how its place in history will be defined.

That is all that I can say in a short introduction for the English-language reader. I am grateful to those of you who hold my book in your hands. As the author, my hope is modest: let my arguments be among the points you reflect upon in drawing your own conclusion.

# Introduction

In December 1917, as perhaps the most decisive year in Russian history was drawing to a close, the Russian poet Vladislav Khodasevich wrote:

> You, my country, and you, its people,
> Will die and come alive again as this year passes.
> Because we have a single truth:
> That every living thing is like a grain of corn.[1]

The thoughts evoked by these lines are very close to me. As one critic said: "There were great hopes of transforming Russia for the better in some mysterious, fantastic way, and poetic daydreams cast a romantic mist over . . . what was actually taking place in the country. Moreover, Khodasevich observed revolutionary events through the prism of biblical wisdom that said that an ear of corn that fell to the ground would bear more fruit as it rotted away.

"Here philosophical wisdom is made concrete, while real life is rendered too poetical: unfortunately, the dying (murdered, executed) person is not revived and only the living 'bear fruit.' The terrible thing is that Russia and its people had to die, not in the artistic sense, but in the most real sense imaginable."[2]

I do not wish to romanticize or mystify my own time in this way. So, does my title, *Out of a Dead End, Into the Unknown: Notes on Gorbachev's Perestroika*, really reflect what was going on in my country, the former Soviet Union, during the *Perestroika* (restructuring) era, from 1985 to 1991?

By the middle of the 1980s, practically everybody in the Soviet Union understood that the country had arrived at a dead end. Some people saw a solution in a return to strict authoritarian rule and highly centralized, disciplined social structure. Some were in favor of cosmetic changes—replacing a few officials here, patching up a few programs there—just to enable us to move forward again. For others it was clear there would have to be far-reaching, even radical reforms. And a few, even then, believed it was essential to change the basic principles by which our society lived and grew.

This explains why Perestroika initially received widespread support as a political course, rightly linked with the name of Mikhail Gorbachev. People supported the idea of getting out of the dead end. But in the course of Perestroika, society began to split up. Perestroika gradually became a road into uncharted territory, into the unknown.

Some people were confused because the guidelines of Perestroika kept changing, as was necessary, to keep things moving and to respond to the dynamics of political life. Others reckoned that Gorbachev's course was leading nowhere except to the collapse of socialist foundations and ideals. And a third group voiced strident disagreement with Perestroika on the grounds that it was clinging too strongly to the past and had not broken decisively enough with the values and traditions of the Soviet period.

Even political observers found it difficult to predict the outcome, because the relationship between these different forces was unclear. So, as we emerged from the dead end, we were plunged into a whirlpool. Even the clarity and predictability of the movement that developed after the collapse of the attempted coup d'état of August 1991 was very soon replaced by new uncertainties—first, the uncertainty over the future of the USSR, and then, with its collapse, the uncertainty surrounding the future of the new states. Then the first steps towards the radical reforms of 1992 presented society with unexpected problems . . . and questions, questions, questions.

Repeating the words of Khodasevich, "You, my country, and you, its people, will die and come alive again as this year passes." I ask myself, which year must I have in mind, the one now behind us, or that which lies ahead?

To answer honestly, I do not know, though, of course, we always want to believe the most frightening and unpredictable times are behind us.

# 1

# Designs in the Arras

History is *one* tapestry. No eye can venture to compass more than a hand's breadth. . . . There is much talk of a design in the arras. Some are certain they see it. Some see what they have been told to see. Some remember that they saw it once but have lost it. . . . Some find strength in the conviction that there is nothing to see. —Thornton Wilder, *The Eighth Day*.[1]

Carving up an organism into its component parts has never resulted, and never will result, in the restoration of health, creative balance or peace. . . . The territory of Russia will boil in never-ending feuds that will develop into worldwide conflicts. That development will be completely irreversible by virtue of the simple fact that states in every part of the world (Europe, Asia, America) will invest their money and extend their commercial interests and strategic plans to the little newly emerging states. . . . Russia will turn into a gigantic 'Balkans,' an eternal source of wars and a great breeding ground for discord. It will become a vat for the whole world into which will be poured the social and moral garbage of all the other countries ('infiltrators,' 'invaders,' 'agitators,' 'spies,' 'revolutionary profiteers,' and 'missionaries')—all the criminal, political and confessional adventurers of the universe. Russia dismembered will become an incurable ulcer on the world. —Ivan Ilyin, *What Does the Breakup of Russia Mean for the World*.[2]

They say that best of all is when people fear and love at the same time; but love does not mix well with fear; therefore, if you have to choose, it is better to choose fear. . . . People are less careful about offending a person who inspires love than one who inspires fear, because love is sustained by gratitude, which people, being stupid, may scorn because of their own interests, while fear is sustained by the threat of punishment, which it is impossible to ignore.

People love their princes according to their own judgment but fear them according to their prince's judgment; therefore it is better for a wise ruler to count on what depends on himself and not on someone else; only it is important that he should not in any event attract upon himself the hatred of his subjects. —Niccolo Machiavelli, *The Prince*.[3]

Perestroika is a pressing necessity that has arisen out of the profound processes taking place in the course of the development of our socialist society. That society is ripe for change—one might say it has suffered enough. Any delay in pursuing Perestroika could lead in the very near future to a deterioration in the situation in Russia.

As with every revolution, there must be no playing about with Perestroika. We must carry it through to the end and mark up successes literally every day, so the mass of the people should themselves feel the effects of Perestroika, that its flywheel should turn faster and the movement should gather speed in both the material and spiritual senses. —M. S. Gorbachev, *Perestroika: New Thinking for Our Country and the World*.[4]

Gorbachev is in my opinion the only person in the country who is afraid of being accused of abandoning his 'principles.' For that he is paying a terrible price. I am not talking now about the causes of his personal tragedy as one of the great Russian reformers. Many people, even those who know our Soviet system well, are determined not to see the objective obstacles that it has come up against. —Aleksandr Tsipko, from an interview in the newspaper *Komsomolskaya Pravda*.[5]

'[Aleksandr Yakovlev], have you never had a feeling that you wanted to write a book about Gorbachev and about yourself?'

'I think it's too soon to be talking about that now. A sort of historical cycle has not yet come to an end, independently even of a man's personal fate. There are also a number of internal contradictions I would not be able to resolve easily. First of all, I am firmly convinced that Gorbachev wanted only good for society and the people. I know that for sure.... But a man's internal convictions do not always coincide with objective logic. Intentions are one thing, the result another.... [Then again,] I do not trust people who produce strictly personal conversations for public discussion. It upsets me even in people's memoirs. A man puts his trust in you and opens his heart to you and you display it to the whole world. Of course, if I find the strength I shall try to write something. But not memoirs and not accusations directed at someone. The Lord preserve me from that. It is more likely to be an attempt at analysis, an interpretation of my times. One thing I can say: Gorbachev is a great and tragic figure.' —Aleksandr Yakovlev, from an interview in *Literaturnaya Gazeta*.[6]

In our day, it seems to me, the dominant way of thinking belongs to the people Thornton Wilder—a writer with a remarkable understanding of history—identified as seeing "only what they have been told to see."

"Who tells them?" the reader asks indignantly. "What right does an author have to humiliate the majority of people in that way?"

I permit myself this assertion only because I'm certain that too little time has passed for anyone to really understand what has happened on the sixth of our planet known until recently as the Soviet Union. Decades of hard and, on both sides, uncompromising ideological and political confrontations have left their mark. The public mind in my country is overstocked with ideologies, causing a great tendency to make one-sided judgments.

Now the last and most powerful state of the socialist commonwealth is no more, and that is a good thing. There is no longer a USSR, and that is wonderful, because it means the last colossus of totalitarianism has fallen. At the demand of the people, self-governing, independent states have been formed on the territory of the former Union, and that is excellent. Or is it? Perhaps it is a catastrophe, because it marks the collapse of a huge country that played a critical role in the geopolitical balance of power. Or because it means the betrayal of the ideals of fathers and grandfathers. Or because abstract values like democracy may not be able to compensate people for the material reality of economic chaos and advancing famine.

I don't claim to have a deep understanding of Perestroika's sources and the processes that led to its end. But I would like to make my contribution to an interpretation of the Perestroika years, a period of such enormous changes in my country and the world. I must attempt this, because few other historians or political scientists have had the advantage of spending more than four years inside the administration that determined the fate of Perestroika itself.

Yes, my senior colleagues saw a great deal more and occupied incomparably more important positions. I did not have real power in my hands. However, this means I have no reason to distort the picture one way or the other and can report what I saw of people with real power in action.

Few people, even in a nightmare, have seen a picture like the one described four decades ago by the brilliant Russian philosopher Ivan Ilyin. He was exiled from Soviet Russia by the Bolsheviks in 1922, along with dozens of other scientists and scholars, and lived and worked for many years in Germany. When the Nazis took power he was forbidden to teach or publish, and he took refuge in Switzerland, where he died in 1954. When you read Ilyin, you are struck by his learning, by his love for his country in spite of the treatment he received, and by his frightening level of intuition.

Of course, we all know that nobody ever learns from history. A prophet is without honor in his own country, and politicians apparently never will understand the mistakes of their predecessors. But as I look today at my tortured and dismembered country, I keep repeating involuntarily, like a prayer or incantation: let new politicians come, let them come soon, and let them be wiser than we were, if only because they will be faced with our errors.

It may seem strange, but in my view the process of renewal in our country included a sort of artificial division between Perestroika within the country and the new thinking in foreign policy. In words, of course, there was continual emphasis on their connection. And I do not have in mind what Eduard Shevardnadze writes about in his book *My Choice,* speaking of the criticisms made against Gorbachev at the January Plenum of the Central Committee in 1991:

> [According to some domestic critics], foreign policy had run too far ahead. It had cut itself off from its popular support. I will permit myself not to agree with this opinion. It was not that foreign policy had run ahead of domestic policy but that domestic policy was lagging behind. Or, more correctly, people were deliberately and quite successfully slowing it down.[7]

No, it is not the problem of synchronizing domestic and foreign policy that I have in mind. Rather, it seems to me that as they established foreign connections, the political leaders of the USSR did not pay sufficient attention to the whole complex of geopolitical and economic interests. It appeared sometimes (right up to 1990 and 1991) that we had forgotten about our ties with Asia and about economic powers beyond Europe, America and Japan. As well, it was puzzling to note the USSR's reaction to the first steps taken towards a market economy in the countries of Eastern Europe. You sometimes got the impression that, apart from the Polish "shock therapy," there was nothing there worth studying. The way we handled our interests in those countries and dealt with the problem of mutual collaboration during and after the dissolution of the socialist commonwealth and the Warsaw Pact was completely incomprehensible. Even with the example of Karabakh already before us, we seemed to brush aside the warning provided by Yugoslavia's tragic experience: we vowed it would not happen to us, but in fact we were sliding into the Yugoslav version. I have my own idea about why that happened.

My version is in its way quite simple, though it has a tragic element: we failed to understand the fact that people at the summit of political power do not become "superpeople." They remain ultimately the same people, with all the strengths and weaknesses nature blessed them with.

Mikhail Gorbachev said more than once, "I am not inclined towards authoritarian rule. Of my own free will I rejected the enormous power that General Secretaries of the Central Committee have traditionally enjoyed. Not a single monarch has had such power." But here is something curious: Having taken state power away from the Politburo and Central Committee and their whole *apparat* (apparatus), Gorbachev did not create any other institutions to administer the state on the basis of law. Having deprived the Soviet Communist Party of functions that were not appropriate to a political party, we did not build alternative institutions capable of correcting the leader's actions. Objectively, then, the scope for arbitrary rule was not reduced but increased. For a time, there was nothing for democracy to rely upon but the personal qualities of Gorbachev himself.

We lacked any state administrative bodies able to carry out decisions independently of the President—and, I must add, independently of his waverings. He had been created by the system and he could not break with it totally. Whatever was part of the system before, the General Secretary said, will continue to be done. It was another matter *how*. Decisions were taken, but there was no one to carry them out.

In my notebooks there are quite a few jottings that bear witness to Gorbachev's understanding of the situation and its seriousness. At various meetings, he formulated his views in an extremely compressed and precise form: "If we don't do this, we shall lose out." "If we don't achieve a breakthrough on this branch of the economy or political life, it will mean a collapse." Orders were issued, often very tough ones. But that was followed by a breakdown in practical work, so many decisions either were not carried out or were delayed. These delays and inadequacies became a chronic feature of political life.

In the passage I've quoted, Machiavelli, with the experience of his age, seems to demonstrate once again that everything in this world is as old as the world. However, human history finds not only its drama but ultimately its optimism in the fact that it is unrepeatable in its repeatability. Roaming among the eternal stories, repeating and forgetting the lessons of the past, history offers practically every new generation the possibility of creating its own history, of establishing itself and displaying its possibilities. From the point of view of an abstract, theoretical understanding of progress, this must be likened to absurdity, to some global variation of the labors of Sisyphus. At the same time, it is nothing other than the right of all new arrivals on this earth to be creative, to display their "egos." Therefore, of course, it is a right not just to successful achievements but also to mistakes, to drama and to tragedy.

If politicians kept Machiavelli's teaching in mind when they took action, they would always be in command. For what do you need in politics apart from an understanding of such problems as the people and power, morals and rights, loyalty and betrayal, ideals and interests, and the ability to apply them practically? Something else, probably. But even this political "minimum" too often develops into misunderstanding and alienation between the politicians and the people, each time in its own peculiar way. And in its own way, so went the course of Perestroika under Mikhail Gorbachev.

No one has produced arguments in favor of Perestroika equal to Gorbachev's own. The whole of his team of supporters and the numerous "Perestroika foremen," of whom there were a great many at the beginning, worked for years in the best Soviet traditions of both science and propaganda, developing and commenting on the General Secretary's ideas. At the time it could not have been otherwise. But there was something more at work.

In the autumn of 1987, when Perestroika had only just begun, a book by Mikhail Sergeyevich Gorbachev called *Perestroika and New Thinking for Our Country and the World* was published simultaneously in the USSR and the US. The author addressed it directly to "the peoples of the USSR, the US and any other country," and said he had written it in order that Perestroika would be properly understood by all.

The book was given a tremendous reception abroad, but evoked surprisingly little attention, to say the least, in the Soviet Union.

I don't believe that in writing this book Mikhail Sergeyevich thought he was writing a catechism of Perestroika. But in our country at that time discussions still took place mainly with reference to what had been said and what was "permitted" by the General Secretary. The disputes which took place between scholars, intellectuals and the tendencies of public opinion that found expression in the press still followed this tradition, even as opinions moved further apart. The book appeared at a time when quarrels about the problems of Soviet history, the place of Perestroika in socialism and the fate of socialism in general were centered on Gorbachev's report, "October and Perestroika: The Revolution Continues," which had marked the seventieth anniversary of the 1917 revolution. But this new book was not received that way—a sign that where future prospects were concerned, people had begun to think for themselves.

However, despite this and despite the policy of *Glasnost* (openness), the Central Committee of the Communist Party at that time continued to lay down the limits of what could be published. The reading public is well aware, for example, of the struggle the magazine *Novy Mir* and its chief editor S. P. Zalygin had to get permission to publish the works of Aleksandr Solzhenitsyn and especially his *Gulag Archipelago*. How many similar cases there were, and how difficult it was to obtain a decision in those days!

For example, on September 9, 1987, L. I. Lavlinsky, editor of the magazine *Literaturnoye Obozreniye* (*The Literary Review*), came to see me. He wanted permission to publish an uncut version of A. M. Gorky's *Nesvoyevremenniye Mysli* (*Untimely Thoughts*)—articles Gorky wrote in 1917 conducting passionate polemics with, among others, Lenin and the Bolsheviks. I took a copy of the text and passed it on "upstairs," as we said in those days. I sent it to one of the top leaders then in charge of ideology—Aleksandr Yakovlev. For a long time I received no reply, though I kept reminding him. Finally he said, "Let us wait a bit, I don't think it will be long." And so, on the 10th of March, 1988, I had to invite Lavlinsky to my office to tell him, "It is considered untimely, let's wait a little."

Eventually, Lavlinsky took it upon himself to publish the material, but that was later. Things changed quickly. At the time, it would have been impossible. The censors would not have let it pass, and people at my level did not hold strong enough views to make a difference. The matter would have been passed from hand to hand up the ladder, reports would have been written, and that would have been the end of it.

But it was one thing when the censors did their reporting, "in the course of duty," so to speak, and another when people did it on their own initiative — reported or "informed" on people. What's more, it was not only the inveterate conservatives and Stalinists who did it. For example, a colleague of mine — in breach of all the rules and regulations — showed me a 1987 report about me, among others, written by a well-known publicist and critic. This critic had proclaimed publicly his "democratic" views in the literary battles of the 1960s, and claimed his "rightful" place in the avant-garde. Luckily, in 1987 times had changed, and to the critic's regret, no practical steps were taken.

I do not tell this story romantically. I simply want to emphasize that my country has found it hard going, but has in fact parted with its unhappy past, by reinterpreting it and learning about Glasnost, pluralism and democracy. The leadership of the country, under Gorbachev, set in motion the machine of democratization because it would have been impossible to undertake the renewal of society in conditions of unanimity. They could not have engaged the sympathy of the masses without struggling with other emergent forces and ideas. After all, the people who started Perestroika had enough potential to last a couple of years, but eventually punishment was meted out for what Mikhail Sergeyevich himself had warned: you must not play about with Perestroika.

On a more personal and human level, I want to emphasize that hard-line ideology is not the exclusive province of conservatives in the tradition of the Soviet Communist Party. It has also appeared among the party's opponents. Today we have seen this with our own eyes. Zviad Gamzakhurdia is only the most striking example—a dissident, a democratic leader in opposition, but a totalitarian once in power. Moreover, if people had carried out a serious analysis instead of listening to the man's own claims, they would have understood earlier that this was not a matter of degeneration but of exposing his real face.

Though not everyone wants to believe it, a certain number of people active in the democratic movements, no less than those who to this very day declare their loyalty to Communist traditions, have been concerned not with seeing that pluralism was maintained but with preventing free thinking—thinking which differed from *their* understanding of the truth.

I have had personal experience with such restrictions. My official duties included analysis of literary developments and links with the writing community, so as soon as I took up my job in the Central Committee I asked them to draw up suggestions to guide the various critics, literary historians and writers. They responded eagerly at the time. They all wanted to make their contribution and to apply their view of life to the process of transformation.

Among those I asked to give their views was V. Kozhinov, a critic who had fallen into disfavor in Brezhnev's days. He was patriotic, but at the same time did not sing the praises of the regime and was critical of what was going on around him. When this became known to the people "upstairs," I was invited to call on a person close to the supreme leadership, simply to explain why I was interested in a critic who held such views. I told them. I named the people with whom I had made contact. The list of names was extremely untendentious. From then, I was kept at a distance.

To this day the unpleasant taste left by that case of "shadowing," is still with me.

I think now of the words (quoted at the beginning of the chapter) spoken in March 1991 by A. S. Tsipko, whom I knew even before Perestroika as an independent-thinking scholar who, incidentally, respected the official doctrine and the official bodies. (I say "incidentally" here because some writers who praise him like to stick a pin in and say: he is a former employee of the Central Committee of the Communist Party. Yes, that is so. But he came into the Central Committee only at a time when it really was the center of Perestroika, where the fate of the country was being decided, where not only things for which the party is today being violently criticized but also things without which we would never have progressed were done. I cannot agree with the current that says Perestroika took root in spite of the Central Committee. No, then it was thanks to the CC. In the Soviet society of those days it could not have been otherwise.)

For an understanding of the ups and downs of Perestroika and the greatness and tragedy of its leader, we must keep in mind the fact that towards the end of 1991 Mikhail Gorbachev had lost his authority and soon would lose power. What distinguished Mikhail Sergeyevich in those years was not just the consistency with which he adhered to socialist ideas and the "principles" about which his opponents kept talking and still talk. There is some truth in this, but only one side of the truth, which they tried in every way to illuminate and exaggerate. In my opinion Gorbachev was not bothered so much by possible accusations of having betrayed socialist ideas—he felt pretty safe on that score—but he did fear accusations of being undemocratic. Centrism, of which he was an advocate, is in principle the most democratic course, but it very often offers grounds for contrary accusations from both right and left.

On February 7, 1992, when he was already retired, Gorbachev took part in a television interview with a number of leading figures in the media. On that occasion he was obliged to reply to a question concerning his lack of willpower. He categorically rejected the charge. And I began to ponder again this particular problem: Was Gorbachev weak-willed? No. Was he capable of assessing other opinions? Yes, though he found it extremely painful to abandon his preferences. Was he a democrat in his way of thinking? Yes. Was he a democrat in his way of acting? Yes, he was. Moreover, he preferred not to assume responsibility for making a decision when there was substantial opposition to it. He had a very specific understanding of democracy under which the opinion of the majority was not regarded as law unless practically everybody was in agreement.

This was the source of the endless explanations and discussions. Why did he behave that way? Was he afraid to assume responsibility? That is not convincing. After all, he took it upon himself to turn the whole country upside down. Was he worried that he had not made the right decisions? That would be difficult to understand, but perhaps that's the way it was.

My doubts and guesses lie where the "I" of the people and the "I" of the politician part company. Gorbachev tried to listen, tried to detect changes in the popular mood, but sometimes they did not reveal themselves, or revealed themselves in such a way that to support them would have meant betraying either his principles or his allies. The result was a vicious circle. Such a circle can be broken only by more straightforward politicians, like the ones that took over from Gorbachev.

In the end, as befits a real democrat, when the situation changed radically after the August coup, he no longer laid stress on the socialist nature of his convictions. He spoke of his adherence to them only when the subject was broached directly. As for his faith in democracy, he remained a democrat in the most complicated and dramatic conditions, even when power was slipping away.

In many parts of the former Soviet Union, leaders who had criticized Gorbachev for his "authoritarian tendencies" have long ago overtaken him in their assertion of authoritarian rule —and not just for the maintenance of order. They have overtaken him in their political declarations and their demands for emergency powers, and in their actual deeds.

"You can't bring back yesterdays, and you can't dodge tomorrows," runs an old Russian saying. I am quite convinced that Mikhail Gorbachev never at any price wanted a return to the old ways, whatever efforts are made to prove the reverse. He was going forward towards tomorrow. He went ahead because he understood what the past was like. But the majority of the people already had a different understanding. Why and when did this division come about?

This is one of the questions posed in a recent interview with Aleksandr Yakovlev, one of the most brilliant politicians who worked with Gorbachev. His reply seems to me a logical reply for a close collaborator who shared Gorbachev's views but was also an independent thinker. But direct involvement with historical events and the central figures of the period is a mixed blessing for the historian and political scientist. Moreover, it is not just a case of "face-to-face you can't see the face," as the poet said. It is not just a matter of the great range for subjective judgments, though that must also not be ignored. The main thing is the psychological and ethical considerations which affect everyone who takes up a pen to write a work in which there is bound to be an element of memoir. Yakovlev acknowledges this.

I share and understand Yakovlev's position, though I do not claim in any way to have been counted among the circle of people closest to Mikhail Sergeyevich Gorbachev. On the political level this can be looked at in two ways: it is bad not to be close when Gorbachev is doing well and good not to be close when Gorbachev is doing badly. (And I do not believe that people ran away from Gorbachev's team only for reasons of principle.) That aside, proximity to the object being analyzed is almost always a plus for a researcher. In this I cannot compare myself with Yakovlev or some other colleagues. But like Yakovlev, I will relate only the part of what I heard and saw which I consider possible to discuss today, for moral reasons. That is what I have in mind when I talk of following the same principles.

I was nearly 40 when, in the summer of 1987, I entered the offices of the Central Committee to work as deputy to the man in charge of the Department of Culture. I dealt with literature and contacts with the Union of Writers. Later—following the reorganization of the Central Committee in 1988, the merging of all the humanitarian departments and, in effect, the abolition of the Department of Culture—I became deputy head of the Ideology department, in charge of work connected with all questions concerning culture and art. For the final two years or so, I worked for Mikhail Gorbachev. From April 1990 to January 1991, I was the General Secretary's assistant. From January 1991 until the dissolution of the USSR and Gorbachev's retirement at the end of that year, I was assistant to the President. I dealt with much the same areas during this period—culture, contact with religious organizations, and in special cases, other branches of humanitarian work.

Today, after the dissolution of the Communist Party of the Soviet Union and the many revelations, both genuine and invented, about its operations, I must address the obvious question: Why did I go to work in the Central Committee?

After all, I had worked previously in the university, then in the Communist youth organization, then in the press and again in the youth movement, and in 1987 I was in my third year as rector of the Literary Institute of the Soviet Union of Writers. Even now, meetings with my fellow teachers and former students at the Institute convince me again that it was a success. The Institute was not too large; it was creative and rather cozy, with quite an open atmosphere. It was very interesting. But no, I decided to make a government career for myself—although by those days this was not such a great advance for a rector.

As I have said, the Central Committee was in those years the center of all work concerned with the renewal of society. The attitude to the party had changed. The party, and especially the Central Committee, was looked to with hope. Politicians like A. Sobchak and S. Stankevich, now well known even in the

West, joined the Communist Party, which they had not done as young men. Everything could be changed through the party—I was quite convinced of that at the time.

There was much that I found surprising in my work at the Old Square, the party's headquarters. Things heard inside were sometimes impossible to understand at close quarters. But I came to understand that in the end everything depends on people, even at the Old Square. And, thanks to the man in charge of the department—Yuri Petrovich Voronov—the climate in our department was very warm.

Voronov was the second reason why I had to make this very difficult decision—to move from an independent job to work in the party *apparat*. Voronov is a good and intelligent person, a remarkably sincere poet, who has not had an easy life. He produced his penetrating poetry out of a childhood spent in Leningrad during the wartime blockade. He suffered during the Brezhnev years of stagnation, for being an honest journalist. Recently he had been editor of the magazine *Znamya,* which had its offices in the Literary Institute's building. I used to go to see him, to chat and drink tea. I saw how he, no longer young and now a sick man, had become involved in Perestroika and had not been able to turn down Gorbachev's invitation to work in the Central Committee. What moral right had I to refuse Voronov's invitation to be one of his deputies? None.

Despite all the twists and turns of history, politics and fate, I am convinced I took the right step in 1987. If there is talk of repentance, as is fashionable now, then I can reproach myself for some things in the Brezhnev era, but I can see nothing during the Perestroika years. And when I meet my now very sick friend Yuri Voronov and we recall the work we did together, I also tell myself confidently that I was right to go help that man. He taught me a great deal, and thereafter life brought me into contact with many remarkable people. I acquired many friends and comrades. What's more, I believe I managed to do quite a lot of good for people, though I cannot be the judge.

That is why I have taken it upon myself to discuss Gorbachev's Perestroika—how it started, and how it ended contrary to his wishes. I discuss it on the basis of personal views and impressions, as well as previously written material. I speak as one of the advisers, assistants and consultants who worked for the President right up to his resignation. As one of them—I claim no more than that.

# 2

# Was Perestroika Really Necessary?

The exposure of the true nature of Stalinism in our country is far from complete. It is, of course, absolutely essential that all the reliable material in existence (including the archives of the NKVD) should be published and that research should be carried out throughout the country. It would be very beneficial for the international authority of the Communist Party of the Soviet Union if the symbolic expulsion of Stalin, the mass murderer, from the Party—which was proposed in 1964 but canceled 'for some reason'—should be carried out and the victims of Stalinism rehabilitated. It is also essential to restrict in every way the influence of neo-Stalinists in the political life of our country.

. . . For today, the key to the progressive restructuring of the state system in the interests of humanity lies in intellectual freedom. This was understood particularly in Czechoslovakia, and we must undoubtedly support their courageous move which is most valuable for the future of socialism and the whole of mankind. . . . I deliberately bring the moral factors into the foreground because, when it comes to the question of ensuring the highest productivity of social labor and the development of productive forces and the question of maintaining a high standard of living for the majority of people, capitalism and socialism have scored a 'draw.'
—A. D. Sakharov, *Reflections on Progress, Peaceful Coexistence and Intellectual Freedom*.[1]

At a certain stage the country started to lose speed, difficulties and unsolved problems began to pile up, and there were signs of depression and other features alien to socialism. . . . Wherein lay the cause of this complicated and contradictory situation?

The principal cause—and the Politburo considers it essential to speak about this quite openly at the Plenum—consisted in the fact that the Central Committee of the Communist Party and the country's leaders, primarily for subjective reasons, were unable to appreciate in good time and in all its aspects the need for change and the danger of allowing a crisis to develop in society or to work out a clear policy for overcoming it and for making the fullest use of the possibilities available in a socialist regime. —M. S. Gorbachev, "Perestroika and the Party's Personnel Policy," January 27, 1987.[2]

The step that was taken was correct, although it was, of course, a revolution from above. In the last analysis such revolutions always turn against the governing *apparat* if it is not able to keep the popular support running in an acceptable channel. It was that *apparat* which began to resist Perestroika, to slow it down and to fight against it, so it literally got stuck in one place. Moreover, the concept of Perestroika had not been properly thought through. It began to look to a large extent like a collection of noisy slogans and appeals.

When I read Gorbachev's book, *Perestroika and the New Thinking*, in the hope of finding in it an answer to the question of how he imagined our path ahead would be, for some reason I did not get the impression that the work was theoretically complete. It is not clear how he sees the restructuring of our house, from what materials he is proposing to rebuild it or what plans he would use. . . . What is surprising is that since April 1985, when Perestroika was first proclaimed, more than four years have passed. But for some reason that period, those four years, are referred to everywhere as the beginning, the first stage, the first steps, and so forth. —Boris Yeltsin, *Confession on a Set Theme*.[3]

There was talk of speeding up the renewal of basic funds and of the reconstruction of factories. Following that it was proposed, on the basis of the new technology, to ensure faster economic growth and the solution of social problems. It was a realistic path to follow, which many of the advanced countries in the West had gone through, reorganizing their industry with new technological systems. . .

But alas, people soon began to improvise in political matters. In the course of choosing tactical ways of developing the economy we made a serious mistake: . . . the well-known slogan of 'acceleration' was proclaimed, promising immediate results. But that is not the way things happen. . . . Then, when the appeal for speeding up economic advance lost its appeal and exhausted its strength, revealing its lack of long-term perspectives and that it was mistaken, we came up against political problems connected with forms of property and then with the market, hoping that it would stimulate the economy. But things turned out quite differently in practice. —Yegor Ligachev, *In The Kremlin and The Old Square.*[4]

These words from prominent figures of the Perestroika era, given here in chronological order, belong to completely different people, brought together and set apart by the passing of time and history. We are ready to consider some of them together today, but between others there has always been a gulf or else one has grown up lately. These statements demonstrate the range of attitudes towards the transformations in the USSR, which had become pressing long before Perestroika.

Today, the leaders of most former union republics have been announced—first in the Belovezha Forest near Minsk (Russia, Ukraine, Byelorussia) and then in Alma-Ata (Kazakhstan, Uzbekistan, Kurgizstan, Tadzhikistan, Turkmenistan, Azerbaidzhan, Moldova). The USSR has dissolved, and as the country itself is in a tense situation socially and politically and between ethnic groups, nobody regards everything the same way. Some are inclined to see positive processes. Others compose a complicated picture in which positive and negative tendencies are interwoven. Still others assess the results of Perestroika as mainly negative. In the middle of the 1980s there was actually a consensus that we could not go on living as we were. But how then were we to live in the future? There was already a variety of views on that issue.

I deliberately began with words written by Andrei Sakharov in June 1968, long before Perestroika. Some people nowadays are inclined to say that it had been clear for a long time that the socialist road had no future, but as this statement demonstrates, that's not how people were thinking—not only the leaders of the Communist Party, but the dissidents as well. History is made, after all, by real people, and they make it as they understand it, in terms of the actual times they are living through.

By the 1970s, politicians and scholars cherished the hope that socialism would get a second wind, that socialist countries might create a system capable of competing with the rest of the world. Indeed, the first steps taken by the Soviet leadership after Gorbachev was elected General Secretary were based on that very idea. The economy was to be modernized by speeding up the introduction of new technology, but there was no talk of a radical transformation of the system. (The words of Yegor Ligachev, leader of a whole tendency in our political life, are an indication of the continued support for such ideas in the Perestroika era and even beyond.)

The reader will have noted where Sakharov put the stress: that in the economy, in a broad social context and in the view of history, capitalism and socialism have "scored a draw." But to "restructure the state system," he added, it would be necessary to get rid of the heritage of Stalinism and create a society of intellectual freedom. Notice that it was a question of restructuring the state, not the whole social system.

That is how things stood until the well-known events in Czechoslovakia. The suppression of the "Prague Spring" left practically no hope at all that there could be any democratic developments under the Brezhnev regime, which was essentially neo-Stalinist. Tougher political controls were followed by an abandonment of economic reforms, and there followed a state of depression and stagnation that lasted for more than fifteen years. The prospect of preserving the attraction of socialist ideas dwindled further and further. Thus, the January 1987 Plenum of the Central Committee of the CPSU marked the beginning of one of the last attempts to make the existing system more democratic and to open up in it fresh possibilities for developing the economy and the country as a whole, as represented in General Secretary Gorbachev's words.

Boris Yeltsin's judgment was made somewhat later. It was written after he had had more than a year to study Perestroika in political opposition to Gorbachev. But at the beginning there were no differences between Gorbachev and Yeltsin. A year before the radical January Plenum, at the carefully prepared 27th Congress of the CPSU, Yeltsin, then first secretary of the Moscow municipal committee of the CPSU, said:

> It is perfectly legitimate to link the drop in the rate of the country's economic development during the last five-year plans with the leadership of the party and the state. The mistakes made by certain people have cost the country too much and have damaged the party's authority and socialism in the world. . . . But the question arises: what were the causes, who is to blame? Who else but we ourselves, members of the Central Committee of the party? It would seem that at times we lose our party vigilance. We must not allow ourselves to be lulled by the permanent political stability the country enjoys. How many times can we repeat the same mistakes, ignoring the lessons of history?[5]

As for the lessons of history, it is true that we have always been very bad at interpreting them and drawing conclusions from them. In some ways, cowardly and opportunist. In some respects just lacking in talent. This huge and extremely wealthy country, so deserving of a better fate, has staggered through the century in a sort of vicious circle, all at the behest of its leaders.

A few words about pre-revolutionary Russia, because the prevailing opinion used to be that before 1917 everything was bad, while now there are some people who would like us to believe that in those days Russia was wildly prosperous.

Yes, at the end of the nineteenth and the beginning of the twentieth century Russia was advancing very rapidly. For example, in the last decade of the nineteenth century the production of iron increased by three times. To achieve the same growth, Germany and the USA needed nearly twenty years, Britain needed more than twenty and France, thirty-five. Between 1890 and 1913, the productivity of labor in Russian industry increased by four times. However, this reflected the fact that Russia had set out on the path of industrial expansion later and had taken full advantage of foreign technology and of foreign capital. At the same time, Russia's share of world industrial output amounted only to 2.6 percent. This compared with France's 6.6 percent, Britain's 12.1 percent, Germany's 15.3 percent, and the USA's 38.2 percent.[6]

By contrast, here are the results achieved during the Soviet period. These are not apologetics, but facts taken from serious scholarly research, based on an alternative analysis carried out by the Siberian scholar G. I. Khanin:

> In spite of the fact that alternative evaluations indicate a considerably slower tempo of industrial growth than do the figures traditionally used, the main indicators of industrial growth of Soviet industry used in our economic literature are confirmed by the alternative assessments. According to the average yearly rate of growth for the period under consideration [1928–1980], Soviet industry outstripped the industry of the overwhelming majority of capitalist countries. Only Japanese industry can bear comparison with Soviet industry for rates of growth. As a result of these rapid growth rates, the Soviet Union's share in world industrial output rose sharply and for several decades the USSR occupied the second place in the world (after the USA) in this category. (Only in the 1980s did Japanese industry succeed in overtaking Soviet industry in volume of output.)[7]

What was going on in this period? In spite of the colossal destruction caused by the First World War, the Civil War, the revolutions, foreign intervention and the enormous economic mistakes made by the early Soviet regime, by 1927 we succeeded, thanks to the NEP (the New Economic Policy, introduced in 1921), in regaining the levels of 1913 in industry and agriculture. Then came the colossal drop in agricultural output which resulted from Stalin's industrialization and collectivization policies, a situation made even worse by the losses suffered in the Second World War. The country's agricultural output reached its 1928 level again only in 1958.[8] But even then, the introduction of further experimental schemes and the personal preferences of each new leader had such an effect on the countryside and so upset its economy that there could be no question of any steady consistent growth of agriculture. There also were no guarantees against routine opposition from the peasants, who were not permitted any control.

The situation in industry has already been referred to. In terms of volume, it looks more than satisfactory. Yes, the USSR had turned into a powerful industrial and military state. The country made a decisive contribution to the defeat of fascism. The USSR was the first to put a man into space. At great effort and expense, military parity was secured with the US. But if we look deeper, the picture we see is quite different:

> Over a long period (1928–1950) industrial production was expanded exclusively on an extensive basis, and intensive factors in that expansion had a negative significance, because resources were used up more quickly than production increased. . . . In the 1950s and 1960s intensive factors played a quite important part in the growth of industrial production, but it was a much smaller part than was played by extensive factors. From the beginning of the 1970s the growth of industrial production again, as in the 1930s and 1940s, assumed an exclusively extensive character.[9]

The average yearly rates of growth of the gross national product were the following: 1960–1970, 7.8 percent; 1971–1974, 5.7 percent; 1976–1980, 4.3 percent; 1981–1985, 3.6 percent. The growth of production per ruble of capital investment amounted in 1970 to one ruble 39 kopecks, in 1975 to one ruble 10 kopecks, and in 1978 to only 81 kopecks. The rate of growth of labor productivity declined steadily: from 13 percent in 1960–1964, to zero in 1980–1984.[10] The roots of the problem were deep down in the economic system. One of the most decisive was the total nationalization of the economy, its increasing centralization, its rigidity and resistance to change. Even in the years of Stalin's industrialization, 60 percent of the national income was redistributed through the state budget. In 1970 the figure was lower than in 1980 (from 55 percent to 67 percent) and in 1985 (69 percent). As a result of the policy pursued in the first years of Perestroika, in 1987 the figure rose to 74 percent.[11]

In the final analysis, a policy based on ideological assumptions, frequently on dogma, and often simply on the subjective views and preferences of the leader, dictated everything in the life of the country—including the economy. This was our misfortune. Gorbachev, I am convinced, knew that very well. He knew it primarily as a local leader who had seen and suffered the inefficiency with which the Brezhnev leadership conducted affairs. His openness, his democratic ways and his new style won people over. People placed tremendous hopes in him and his new approach to politics. He gave the impression of a man who had tremendous potential and who was held down by "rules of the game" that prevailed to 1985.

I remember well, soon after the May 1982 Plenum at which the USSR food program was approved, hearing Mikhail Gorbachev reply to questions at a meeting with leaders of the media. Gorbachev was at the time already a member of the Politburo and a secretary of the Central Committee in charge of agriculture. That was the first occasion when I saw and listened to Mikhail Sergeyevich. (On previous occasions, when I had been able to observe him sitting on the platform at various large gatherings amid the Brezhnev leadership, when everybody remained silent, it was impossible to understand who was who.) Gorbachev spoke about the results of the Plenum and the essence of the food program. He seemed quite at ease. He spoke practically without any notes, which was quite unusual in those times. Nevertheless, I would not have remembered that occasion had it not been for one episode.

One of the journalists asked if everything planned for the Plenum had been approved, if Gorbachev was satisfied, and if he considered the decisions taken sufficient to create the conditions for improving agriculture. I think there was also a request for more precision about the RAPO (local agro-industrial unions), which were regarded as the organizational basis for the new agrarian policy. Gorbachev's reply surprised me and several of my comrades by its frankness and a sort of sincere-sounding disappointment. Of course, he said, not everything that had been prepared and that we had requested had been approved. This was a very unusual statement for

1982, because if a Politburo member's suggestion had not been approved, the proposal must have been "killed" higher up. For us, who otherwise did not really know the balance of forces, it was a hint that the General Secretary himself was not willing to undertake radical measures.

I have not made this digression in order to set off something unpleasant for Gorbachev today. On the contrary, it is only by remembering that period of stagnation that we may understand the enormous strength it took to begin such a sharp turn in the life of the country. In this connection, with a recognition of the need always to remember the exact and not the edited version of history, I was amazed to read the edited texts of articles and speeches by Gorbachev in the pre-Perestroika period—in which kind words addressed to Brezhnev have disappeared. Why? History was what it was, and no politician could have survived at the top if he had stood out from the crowd. There is a very apt saying among the people: "Don't go into another's monastery with your own rules." And the monastery in those days was Brezhnev's.

Society was gasping for breath. We could not go on living like that, but to strive for a renewal was not a fate for the wise. I believe that was the mood in society of an absolute majority of thinking people. It was only a question of what changes should take place and who was going to have the courage to start.

Society was pregnant with changes. Soon after the beginning of the five-year plan that followed the 26th Congress of the CPSU (February–March 1981) the leaders of the party and state began to die one after the other, due to their age or state of health. You can't deceive the ordinary people, and they very soon christened the new five-year plan the "Three P's"— *pyatiletka pyshnykh pokhoron*—"the five-year plan of the fancy funerals." Of fourteen Politburo members, by the spring of 1985, six had passed away. They buried three general secretaries—Brezhnev, Andropov and Chernenko—and many high-placed ideologues and underlings.

Today, when the memoirs of several party leaders have been

published, we already know about the struggle that went on behind the scenes and the relation of forces in the Politburo. Nevertheless, it seems to me that by no means all points have been made correctly and in context. People at the highest levels of the regime were probably wondering how changes would come about and where they would lead us. But all we know from documents is that all the principal politicians in 1985 (the leaders of the CPSU, Gorbachev's future opposition and the future leaders of the democratic movements) thought in terms of modernizing socialism and of a revolution from above.

The "insights" that are to be found sometimes in the memoirs prompt my doubts. They contain too much of subsequent experience transferred to the beginnings of Perestroika. After all, even Boris Yeltsin, the most prominent and authoritative opponent of the CPSU, spoke in 1987 quite differently from the way he spoke a couple of years later. We should not forget, as Aleksandr Yakovlev pointed out in a television interview in the autumn of 1991, that he had criticized Yeltsin at an October 1987 Plenum of the Central Committee—for having denounced Gorbachev from *conservative* positions.

The changes were inevitable. A leader of the reform movement was emerging.

# 3

# Why Gorbachev?

So time is the first principle and source of political renewal. No government that does not conform with the spirit of the time cannot hold out against its all-powerful action. Now—that is at the end of the first decade of the last century—the time was ripe for reforms. Ranks and honors had lost their charm and the reason for this was obvious: when reason begins to recognize the price of freedom it sweeps aside with scorn all what we might call the children's toys that it played with in its infancy.

These objections came about mainly because elements in our government are not yet sufficiently educated and the minds of the people who compose it are not sufficiently impressed by the absurdity of the present state of affairs to recognize the need for constructive changes. Consequently it will take more time . . . and then they will themselves wish them to be carried out. —M. M. Speransky, *Jottings in Various Years*.[1]

You see, gentlemen, here they are proposing the destruction of the existing state system and that we, in the midst of other strong and powerful peoples, should reduce Russia to ruins so as to build on those ruins a new fatherland of which we have no idea. I believe that, in the second millennium of its life, Russia will not collapse. I believe she will revive, will make a better contribution and advance.

In Western states this required decades. We are offering you a modest but sure road. The opponents of the state system would like to choose the path of radicalism, of emancipation from Russia's historical past, to be freed from our cultural traditions. They need great shocks—but we need a Great Russia! —P. A. Stolypin in the State Duma [parliament], May 10, 1907.[2]

Could Gorbachev have broken out of that vicious circle in 1985? At that time could anybody else in his place turn to his comrades in the CPSU and say: friends, maybe we are not heading in the right direction at all? Perhaps we should liberate the economy from its ideological chains, destroy the state's monopoly of property, stop subsidizing unprofitable enterprises, permit competition, let the peasants own their land, make big cuts in military spending and carry out the conversion of the armament industry? — The reply is obvious. That could not have been proposed in 1985. Such a party leader would have expelled immediately from the CPSU and escorted without delay to a madhouse. — From a collective monograph prepared by contemporary Soviet historians and political scientists.[3]

My first meeting with Gorbachev made a deep impression on me, both on the personal level and when it came to business. In April 1985 the new master in the Kremlin was still little known even in the Soviet Union. After my meeting with him journalists asked me what sort of a person he was. I replied literally the following: 'If anybody can change that country, he is the man!' — F. Wilgelm Kristians, *Roads to Russia*.[4]

Suddenly there was a call from Gromyko. On a day like this! Of course I didn't for a moment doubt that the call was about that day's Plenum of the Central Committee of the CPSU, and about the question of the election of a new General Secretary.

'Yegor Kuzmich, who are we going to choose as General Secretary?'

I realized that, in asking me such a straight question, Gromyko knew for sure the sort of reply he would get, and he was not mistaken.

'Yes, Andrei Andreyevich, it's not an easy question.' I replied. 'I think you will have to choose Gorbachev. You have, of course, your own opinion. But since you ask me, that's what I think.' Then I added: 'I know that is the way many first secretaries of provincial parties and members of the Central Committee are thinking.'

'I am also thinking of Gorbachev. In my opinion he is the most suitable person, the one with the best prospects.' Andrei Andreyevich seemed to be thinking aloud. — Yegor Ligachev, *In The Kremlin and The Old Square*.[5]

*M. S. Gorbachev*: 'I cannot agree with what people sometimes say, that the policy of reviving socialism is linked personally with the name of Gorbachev. That would be contrary to the truth. The development of a new policy is a reflection of the fact that there existed in Soviet society and in the Soviet people a general understanding of the necessity for change. In other words, if there had not been Gorbachev there would have been someone else. Our society was ripe for change and the necessity for change cut its way through.'

*G. Chiaromonte*: 'Did you not give thought to these problems when you worked in Stavropol?'
*M. S. Gorbachev*: 'That can be said about a lot of comrades who were working in the provinces. We saw the real processes that were taking place in society, and we felt that it couldn't go on like that.' —From an interview in the newspaper *Unita*, May 18, 1987. G. Chiaromonte is one of the leaders of the Italian Communist Party and editor-in-chief of the newspaper.[6]

Why was it Mikhail Sergeyevich Gorbachev that history chose as the leader fated to become the country's next great reformer, at a difficult and critical turning point in its development?

Nowadays, when speaking about Gorbachev, people often repeat what has been said about the frequently tragic fate of reformers in Russia. In the course of the thousand-year long history of the Russian state there have been quite a few major politicians who have made a deep impression on its history. Some of them, on account of the scale and results of their work, as well as the methods by which they brought about their reforms, deserve to be called revolutionary. But if in the case of, say, Lenin, the term "revolutionary" seems logical, in the case of Peter the Great, for example, it is not usually used. Yet Peter the Great did not merely carry out reforms. He inherited the Tsar's crown and turned it into the crown of the Russian Empire. While keeping the dynasty in power, he in effect replaced the nobles at the helm of the ship of state with the service gentry and opened the corridors of power to the factory owners and the merchants—that is, to the emerging bourgeoisie.

Reformers are people who, however profound the changes, either did not plan or permitted, contrary to their own ambitions, results that are primarily typical of a change of forces at the top. A certain simplification of historical parallels makes it possible to put these names alongside one another—M. M. Speransky, P. A. Stolypin and M. S. Gorbachev.

Speransky (1772–1839), one of the most important of Russian reformers, was born into the family of a village priest. He had exceptional ability, and when he was only a little over 20 he was picked out by the Holy Synod and given a career in the government service. In 1799, in the reign of Paul I, he was already in charge of the office of the Procurator-General, through whose hands all the most important state affairs passed. In the reign of Alexander I and later of Nicholas I, Speransky was in charge of preparing projects and putting into practice the most important state reforms. He was responsible for drawing up plans for the reform of the state administration—"A Collection of Laws of the Russian Empire" and "A Complete Collection of Laws." But Speransky was the victim of intrigues. He spent six years in exile, followed by a slow return to power, as Governor-General of Penza in Siberia, and was properly recognized just before his death. Speransky's idea of a constitutional limit on absolutism thus received no support.

Even more tragic was the fate of Peter Arkadevich Stolypin (1862–1911). His career took off more slowly, but at 44 he became chairman of the Council of Ministers of Russia—Prime Minister. In Soviet histories his name is linked with practically nothing but the suppression of the first Russian revolution in 1905. But his most important work was in agrarian reform and the idea of an all-embracing social reformation of Russia. Stolypin's reforms aimed at accelerating the growth of capitalism and increasing the country's strength and its military might. Of course, if these had been successful, the idea of revolution would have dropped from the Russian agenda, so the revolutionaries made repeated attempts to assassinate Peter Arkadevich. In the course of one of these attempts 25 innocent people were killed and his three-year old son and fourteen-year old daughter were injured. The rebels finally succeeded in killing Stolypin on September 1, 1911, in the Kiev opera house. After his death his reforms were doomed. But even if he had not been killed, according to the historians, he would have been dropped and sent into retirement. The people around the Tsar loathed reformers.

So you see, all Russian reformers have found themselves in this position: they tried to change the situation, to carry out reforms by passing new laws and limiting the absolute power of the monarch, so that the laws could make it possible for life to advance along new lines. But the Tsars, or the people close to them, did away with the laws and nullified the half-measures that had been achieved. In Russia the law has always been subordinated to personal power.

What has this to do with Gorbachev? He had nobody above him. True, but the trouble was that there was no law above Gorbachev. When he was forced to resign, contrary to the Constitution and the laws, there turned out to be yet another power — the collective power and will of the leaders of the former union republics. With regard to Gorbachev the reformer they played the absolutist part, setting themselves above the law. When the man behind the reformist laws started to interfere, they showed him the door.

Very well. But what connection do these thoughts have with the problem of why it was Mikhail Gorbachev who was chosen by history for the role of the leader of Perestroika? In my opinion, a very direct connection — through the objective laws of Russian history.

There are laws to history, to cultural development, to a particular state system. There are also juridical laws that form the legal basis of the state. These overlap, have an influence upon each other, but are far from always coinciding. So, according to the laws of Russian history, including the Soviet period, it was impossible for anyone with a different biography than one like Gorbachev's to rise to a key position.

A person could not be appointed to the leading role in the country who was not a member of the Politburo of the Central Committee of the CPSU, the supreme political body in the system as it was made up in 1985. An official could not "infiltrate" into the Politburo if he did not have behind him the appropriate political, and more precisely *Party*-based career. Finally, a man who did not have the ability, at least hypothetically, to carry out the new policy could aspire but could not ultimately count on being elected General Secretary.

There are today quite a few memoirs recounting how Gorbachev came to the fore and was elected General Secretary, by Yegor Ligachev, the man who was in charge of personnel matters and organizational questions in the Central Committee; by Victor Grishin, one of the most influential members of the Politburo and a possible candidate himself, backed by the "old guard"; by Eduard Shevardnadze, a candidate member of the Politburo and first secretary of the Communist Party in Georgia; by Boris Yeltsin, a man who at that time had seen what a provincial leader could see from a distance. With all the differences in detail, they all agree on one thing: there was no real alternative to Gorbachev.

Gorbachev was supported by Andrei Gromyko, who thus made, it seems to me, a decisive contribution to Gorbachev's election as General Secretary. He was the most authoritative and experienced leader at the time. He was a leader in Stalin's day. From 1943 he occupied the most important diplomatic posts; from 1957 he was continuously Minister of Foreign Affairs; and from 1973 he was a member of the Politburo. Gromyko had seen and knew the West. This was probably why, although he belonged to the older generation of top leaders, he was better able than anyone else to think in different terms from his colleagues, as he showed in his speech honoring the new General Secretary after Gorbachev's election.[7]

Here I will make another digression. The first time I found myself unable to understand Gorbachev on a personal level was in 1989, at the time of Gromyko's death. Andrei Andreyevich, who had been Chairman of the Presidium of the Supreme Soviet—the nominal head of state—had since the autumn of 1988 been in retirement, since he was over 80. His position was taken over by Gorbachev, who remained at the same time leader of the party. When he died, Gromyko was given a modest funeral at the Novodeviche cemetery, as the new Soviet leadership had put an end to funerals at the

Kremlin wall, which I think was a correct move. But Gorbachev did not even attend the funeral of this man, who had given Gorbachev such strong support in advancing his career. I don't know what relations between them had been like towards the end, but that has no importance for me in this case. I have always taken the view that we are all equal in the eyes of God and that to pay a last tribute to the deceased is an ancient Christian custom and a national tradition.

But let us return to the Spring of 1985.

All sorts of people saw in Gorbachev a candidate for the post of General Secretary, not only officials of the CPSU. It has been written about, as cited above, by F. Vilgelm Kristians, Chairman of the Supervisory Council of the Deutsche Bank. There are a great many similar accounts. And to those who in hindsight wanted to appear more intelligent and far-sighted than they were in the mid-1980s, I would repeat the words of A. Tsipko: "I do not think that if Yeltsin had been in Gorbachev's place in March 1985 he would have succeeded in doing more for democracy. In those actual political conditions, with his character, he would have broken his neck in a couple of months."[8]

So, as in the past, by the 1980s the country was facing the necessity for change. It could be led only by a man who had been brought up in the system, supported by it and not alien to it, but possessed the qualities of a reformer. But there also must be caution and flexibility. Otherwise you can break your neck, and ruin the plan of reform altogether, no matter how ready the country is.

Yes, there have been a great many books and articles welcoming Mikhail Gorbachev and his policies in similar terms. But not only in the Soviet Union and in the former union republics, but also in the West—until recently almost universally infected by "Gorbymania"—there are now beginning to appear not just critical but bitterly anti-Gorbachev publications. The process of interpreting Perestroika is becoming ever more complicated.

Among the books about Gorbachev there are quite a few in which the authors ask the natural question: Why did he become the leader of the process of change? I will take one of those that have appeared recently, Mikhail Heller's *The Seventh Secretary: The Rise and Fall of Mikhail Gorbachev*. It contains a great deal of factual material, with interesting and often accurate observations. But it also contains an exceptionally large number of epithets and judgments that demand comment. In this book, Gorbachev's career from the days of his youth is analyzed, or rather commented on, from a standpoint which rejects the Communist system and its ideology, its tradition of the *nomenklatura* appointing people to official positions, and even Gorbachev's personal qualities. There is no reason of course why a historian should like everything. But what is important, after all, is not to make judgments, not to reward with epithets, but to understand. From these standpoints, the career of Mikhail Sergeyevich was a normal one for leaders of his generation: It is what it is.

At the same time there is in Gorbachev's career one period that must not be underestimated—his years as a student at Moscow University. I agree with what Heller says in argument with Zdenek Mlynar, a fellow student of Gorbachev's and one of the future leaders of the "Prague Spring." Of course, there are no grounds for depicting the young Mikhail Gorbachev as a persuaded anti-Stalinist, almost ready to join the ranks of the dissidents.[9] But one must not fail to emphasize the fact that none of the Soviet leaders at the beginning of the 1980s had a sound humanitarian education, while Gorbachev obtained at Moscow University the best legal training that a young man could have in the Soviet Union. Mikhail Sergeyevich thus had an excellent potential for a serious intellectual and cultural future in Moscow.

At the same time we must not underestimate the importance of this circumstance. Moscow and its university were being planted in Gorbachev's case in very rich soil. A proud young man had come up from the provinces to study and to make his mark in society. Behind him were not only hands bearing the callouses of hard labor in the fields but also a childhood spent in territory occupied by the fascists. For a person of his age he had already seen many things, and "life under the Germans," as people used to say, was a good reason for being suspicious. Bewilderment and a growing internal protest against the most odious features of Stalinism was rather natural in the intellectual development of a person with such a youthful biography.

Moscow and the university were later preserved for him as a point of reference in his work both in the youth movement and in the party, but he had already been in incomparably greater proximity to the country's real problems. The sufferings of the people were always felt much less in the relatively well-fed city of Moscow, which served as a sort of shop window for foreigners. Conditions in the provinces were very different.

In his poem "The University of Khazar" Yevgeni Yevtushenko wrote about another man from the Russian Provinces who turned the country upside down. His poem was about Lenin, but it provides a good basis for understanding Mikhail Sergeyevich's student years in Moscow:

> *Provincial life is fine*
> *For saving a man from despair*
> *And even if you are a city man*
> *To love the provinces is no great sin*
> *Moscow and Petersburg — don't boast too much*
> *About your charms — We thank you for them*
> *But don't forget how many wise men*
> *Have come out of provincial life*
> *To help our country spread its wings.*

Not so long ago, the well-known sculptor and former Soviet dissident Ernst Neizvestny, recalling his youth in the 1950s, made an interesting remark about his friends and fellow students of those years: some had graduated to become dissidents and others to become Speranskies, reformers in the state administration. (Speransky himself had had very close relations with the future Decembrists, the first Russian revolutionaries.) As I understand it, Gorbachev absorbed the maximum possible amount of free thinking available in Moscow University in the 1950s, the years immediately following the death of Stalin and preceding the 20th Congress of the CPSU, the first stage in the exposure of Stalinism. The road to becoming a reformer has its logic, and was certainly logical for him.

Nobody who has met Gorbachev can have any doubts that he is a well educated and highly cultured man with a strong personality. I remember very well a long conversation I had with the writer Viktor Petrovich Astafyev in June, 1988. He called on me after having had an interview with Gorbachev. He did not go into great detail, reckoning apparently and quite rightly that there was no reason to recount in detail what had taken place at a meeting face to face. But I recall two things from what he told me. "You know," Astafyev said, "I was a little confused at the outset. I wanted to say this and that and to decide something, but he, Gorbachev, just went on talking and talking. Well, never mind, I also like to talk. And so we chatted, interrupting one another." The other thing Astafyev noted, with a sort of genuine joy and a devilish look flashing in his eyes: "But it's a good thing that at last we have a clever *muzhik* who has come to rule Mother Russia!" And in the word *muzhik* one could detect something worldly, dependable and comprehending — in a word, one of us.

Or take Gorbachev's interview with one of the best-known people in the West, the evangelical preacher Billy Graham, on July 12, 1991. That was a remarkably rich exchange. Graham talked about faith and Christ, about peace and the part played by people with faith in securing happiness on earth; he recalled earlier meetings with Gorbachev and the way they had sung together "Moscow Nights" with Van Cliburn at the

Yegorov and others welcome Billy Graham, shown fourth from left, before meeting with Gorbachev in Moscow.

Dialogue in the Kremlin: Billy Graham and Mikhail Gorbachev. Vladimir Yegorov sits to the left of Gorbachev.

piano, and his encounters with leading politicians like Konrad Adenauer and Ronald Reagan. Mikhail Sergeyevich pondered the subject of what exactly faith was, what humanity could hope for in the future, and about the paths along which civilization would advance. Then they took their leave of each other. I was amongst those who guided our American guests out of the office. As we walked down the long Kremlin corridors Billy Graham said, "I have been talking to a great man, the greatest of all those I have met." And he repeated those words again, after saying a prayer, at the entrance to the residence of the Soviet President. This made a tremendous impression on me.

Of course, in the extremely complicated situation following the collapse of the USSR, this kind of judgment may evoke categoric disagreement and protest. There are grounds for having such feelings and it would be hypocritical to assert otherwise. But this is not rudimentary, and not a survival of conservatism. In fact, it is always rather risky to use the epithet "great" with reference to politicians. There are too many conflicting interests and emotions in politics. For that reason I will be more precise: in defining any politician, it is in my view more accurate to arrange them according to importance, not in categories of good or bad. That is how I see the problem of judging the Gorbachev legacy.

# 4

# The Philosophy of Renewal

We are obliged to admit a radical change in our whole attitude to socialism. —V. I. Lenin, *About Cooperation*.[1]

The people were in the past aware of the injustice of the social system, based on the oppression and exploitation of the working people, yet they bore meekly and humbly their life of suffering. But the time came when they did not wish to suffer any longer and the whole structure of the popular mind was tipped upside down. This is a typical process. Meekness and humility can turn into ferocity and fury. Lenin could not have carried out his plan for revolution and the seizure of power without a revolution having taken place in people's minds. That revolution was on such a scale that the people, who had lived by irrational beliefs and submitted to an irrational fate, suddenly went almost out of their minds in the course of rationalizing the whole of life and believed in the possibility of rationalization with nothing irrational left, and put their faith in the machine instead of God. . . . Such sudden switches are possible in people's minds. —N. A. Berdyaev, *The Origin and Meaning of Russian Communism*.[2]

Westernism in its various forms remained the dominant trend among the Russian intelligentsia right up to the revolution. This life on two planes, this duality between their political homeland—Russia—and their spiritual homeland—the West—was in itself a tragedy. . . . Western culture was sufficient to enable people to break away from Russia and learn to loathe its way of life and faith. But there was no way to replace the emptiness that had come about.

Bolshevism is a phenomenon reflecting an even deeper collapse of the intelligentsia and is at the same time a form of revolutionary activity by the truly proletarian sections of the people, repeating the nihilism of the 1860s. Totally devoid of . . . in general, ethical ideals, only in its maximalism and its thirst for a radical transformation of the world did it correspond to the vague religious demands of the Russian people.—Georgi Fedotov, "The Fate of Our Intellectual Culture."[3]

Modern political democracy—if it is limited to a strictly political sphere—is not capable of overcoming the consequences of the economic insignificance of the average individual. But neither is a purely economic approach—such as the nationalization of the means of production—sufficient. 'Socialism' has become a sort of magic word which even the German Nazis used for their tactical ends, but at the moment it is Russia I have in mind. In spite of the nationalization of the means of production the word 'socialism' became in Russia a misnomer because in Russia the greater part of the population is manipulated by the all-powerful bureaucracy; even if such an administration were capable of acting in the economic interests of the majority of the people, it would inevitably obstruct the development of freedom and individualism.—Erich Fromm, *Escape From Freedom*.[4]

The society which took shape in the years of the Stalin terror cannot be called either socialist or capitalist, or state-capitalist, or even feudal. Those are all terms that apply to the emergence and development of western, 'European' civilization . . . in which we did not find a place. It would be more correct to describe our society as 'modernized Asiatic,' what Marx called the 'Asiatic form of production,' 'the primary (archaic) social formation,' only somewhat changed in appearance through the influence of industrialization. If the classical 'Asiatic despotism' took shape on the basis of agricultural production, combining it with a modern industrial foundation strengthened its despotic qualities many times over and produced in the end totalitarianism of the Stalinist type. 'Real socialism' turned out in practice to be a purely 'Asiatic' way of building an industrial society, employing for that purpose the use of force by the state and forced labor not justified economically.—V. M. Mezhuev, "Socialism as an Idea and as a Reality."[5]

Life and its dynamism dictate the necessity for further changes and transformations, the achievement of a qualitatively new state in society, in the broadest sense of the word. It is primarily a question of the scientific and technological renewal of industrial production and the achievement of a higher level of labor productivity in world terms. It is also a question of perfecting relations in society, and in the first place economic relations. It means profound changes in the field of labor and the material and intellectual conditions in which people live. It also means activating the whole system of political and social institutions, the extension of socialist democracy and self-government by the people.—M. S. Gorbachev, April 23, 1985.

Everything must be changed: the regime, the federation, the economy, the attitude to property and the status of the individual. . . . We need a mighty regrouping of political forces.—M. S. Gorbachev, August 23, 1991.[6]

One of the most difficult and painful problems for Soviet society and for our politicians in the Perestroika years was to define the strategy or, if you like, the philosophy behind the transformation.

In fact the overwhelming majority of the Soviet population supported the changes initiated in 1985. Towards the middle of 1986, however, Gorbachev himself spoke in alarm about opposition and misunderstanding of Perestroika: "There are still among us, of course, people who find it difficult to accept the word 'Perestroika' and sometimes even to pronounce it. . . . People sometimes ask what is this strange thing—Perestroika—what's it for, what do you eat it with, this Perestroika? We are all in favor of it, but we don't know what to do with it."[7]

There was even more alarm in his voice in Krasnodar in September of the same year, as he attempted to explain the concept of Perestroika, referring to Lenin and the experience of history, and to assure people that the leadership knew what it was doing: "We now have a truly scientific and well thought out—I would even say deeply thought out—political line—a strategy for the acceleration of the social and economic development of the country."[8]

Even in October 1986, speaking to the All-Union Conference of professors of social science—people who dealt professionally with the theory and practice of socialism—Gorbachev presented no concepts to fundamentally revise his developmental strategy. He did not go beyond the ideas of April 1985, quoted at the beginning of this section, when he spoke of the need to achieve "a qualitatively new state of Soviet society." The idea was still to achieve this new state without introducing any radical reforms, asking the social scientists to concentrate on working out a "reliable scientific way of guaranteeing practical measures for perfecting social relationships in developing socialism."[9] Of course, by comparison with earlier times, there was a lot of innovation, a great deal that was progressive and down-to-earth. But even among such an orthodox audience of teachers and sociologists there was already talk in the corridors, complaints that there were no breakthroughs. Once again, everything was based on the mantra, "Improve, perfect and modernize." I remember very well the protest by the scholars, at that time still only behind the scenes.

Criticism spread especially quickly among writers and artists. At the time I was teaching a course on the theory and practice of socialism to writers taking the advanced literary courses of the Union of Writers at the Literary Institute. Then, it was still possible to explain Perestroika rationally to these writers, but emotionally and psychologically they would not accept such theories. They were accustomed to being close to the real world, to being observant and more inclined to think than to believe. Their reactions helped me free myself from dogma and ideology. It was not so easy for me, and I am grateful to that special audience for their insight. It would not be long before practically the whole of society would refuse to live under the control of dead theories.

But criticism of Gorbachev and Perestroika at that time was muffled, and couched in allegorical language, since people were only just beginning to talk of openness as a policy. Moreover, it was personified in those years by the emerging conservative, anti-Perestroika forces. There was no radical criticism yet. All our radicals followed the General Secretary, the reformer, and, as our people say, "looked him in the mouth" and quoted him when there was a dispute.

The criticisms of Gorbachev and Perestroika were concentrated to a large extent on the need for an idea of renewal. But both the General Secretary and the party leadership as a whole were then feeling very confident. Criticism of the society we were living in went ever deeper and further. At the January 1987 Plenum of the Central Committee, for the first time, Perestroika as a policy took precedence over the policy of acceleration. Deeper causes had to be found for the signs of crisis and increasing contradictions. But people found it difficult, not only to produce a realistic policy but also to reinterpret their Soviet experience.

We keep on repeating that Perestroika started in April 1985. But that is an exaggeration. Look what Gorbachev himself said in February 1987, nearly two years later:

> So far we have mainly been preparing for Perestroika, working out its strategy and indicating the main courses to follow. . . . Now we must get Perestroika going in practical terms. What was begun in 1987 will be in many ways decisive, because today the fate of Perestroika is being decided and the foundations for accelerated development are being laid.[10]

There was certainly some truth in Boris Yeltsin's complaint, "For some reason this period, four whole years, is called the beginning, the first stage, the first steps, and so forth." It reproduces accurately the mood of those years—first one year goes past and then another and it's still the beginning, a preparation. When do we get down to practical work?

In this particular stage of Perestroika, the political course and personal inclinations of Mikhail Gorbachev began to emerge more clearly. This, it seems, was the essence of it:

> We shall continue along the path of Perestroika steadfastly and consistently, along the path of democracy and reform—steadfastly and consistently, but we shall not skip stages in the process. We shall not permit any adventurous moves . . . but neither shall we permit conservatism. . . . We shall be very cautious and conscious of our responsibility. We have at our back a huge country and a great people. We cannot permit anybody to treat politics as a game.[11]

That was said at the end of 1987, and President Gorbachev continued to hold those views to the end. However, when it came to be applied in practice, decisions based on this analysis required meticulous answers to questions like: What moves are adventurous? What is conservatism? What is ripe and what is not ripe for practical application? Future developments showed that the main mistakes were made here. The situation in the country and the popular mood were evolving in ever greater disharmony with the official course of action.

If we remain realists we have to say that the philosophy of Perestroika was formulated gradually, not without contradictions, and that much changed in the approach to the reforms. But it is also a fact that, as he developed and changed and evolved in his understanding of society, Gorbachev remained true to his principles and convictions and to the socialist path. Moreover he remained for a long time an advocate of developing an integral concept of social transformation. In such an important policy document as his report to the 19th Conference of the CPSU on June 28, 1988—a conference that historians and politicians rightly regard as one of the key stages of Perestroika and the democratization of Soviet society—Gorbachev said, "We need objective and scholarly research into such problems of Perestroika as economic reform, the reorganization of the political system, democratization, humanistic reform, relations between the peoples, the new political thinking and many others. In other words, society, which is moving towards a qualitatively new state, needs an integral conception of development, a vision of the dialectics of the processes, a need to take account of the pluralism of opinions and the formulation of scientifically founded perspectives."[12] Right up until the CPSU started drawing up new programmatic documents in the summer of 1991, he tried to forge a contemporary conception of socialism.

The documents the CPSU produced for that 1991 deadline were essentially not Communist, but social-democratic, as social democracy is understood in the West. But after the August coup in 1991 the CPSU was dissolved and its latest policy documents became the property of history. All the same, if we simply draw up a list to identify the problems, questions and ideas that ultimately constituted the philosophy of renewal, it is quite a substantial list. And I should remind the foreign reader that practically nothing of what follows entered the theoretical or political arsenal of the CPSU in such a form. Without being aware of this it is impossible to understand properly either the place or the significance of Perestroika in my country's history.

From a one-sided understanding of the essence of socialism, we progressed to the recognition of every people's right to make its own path within the socialist framework, according to its own national and cultural traditions. The CPSU and the USSR finally abandoned their practice of imposing their own ideas of what was good and what was bad in the social system. This transformation laid the theoretical and political foundation for the liberation of both the countries of Eastern Europe and the former union republics of the USSR.

It was of tremendous importance, not only for the international situation but also for the country's internal development, that general human values were given priority over class and other factors. The new thinking gained recognition because it was based on the primacy of human rights and a rejection of the conflicts between military blocs and the idea of the "enemy." The key thesis here was that we are living basically in a single, integrated world in which it is essential to assert the principles of freedom of choice so that the forces of politics take priority over the force of weapons. The strategy was based on guarantees of security, not through an extremely high but an extremely low level of armaments in strategic balance, with nuclear and other weapons of mass destruction excluded from politics. In the final analysis it was a question of freeing interstate relations from ideology and encouraging their development by the norms of civilized exchange and human morality.

The philosophy of Perestroika took ever more clearly the

form of a philosophy of transformation based on such principles as recognition of the equal rights of different forms of property, including private property, and the necessity to found economic activity on market relations. There could have been no thought of such conclusions before Perestroika—as was the case with the democratization of society, the rule of law, the multiparty state, the rejection of ideology, the recognition of pluralism, genuine freedom of speech and religion, and so forth. Glasnost, as a phenomenon and as a quality of political life, was a locomotive for ever more radical transformations.

The new social role of science and culture, too, gradually became assured. The intelligentsia, the most active of all sections of society that supported Perestroika—writers and artists, journalists and scholars—gradually became the leaders of popular thought. They not only contributed to a new understanding of the past, of historical truth, or of humanist ideas; they also helped to extend the limits in studying the country's present and future. Admittedly, they also made their not inconsiderable contribution to the growth of nationalist and separatist tendencies. But without an increase in national self-consciousness and without a new reading of the difficult and historically confused relationships between the peoples and the republics it was impossible to have scope for a truly free and democratic development.

This list could be continued, but enough has been said to indicate the scale of the breakthroughs achieved during Gorbachev's rule. Yes, he remained to the end, I repeat, a supporter of the socialist path. He spoke about this frankly and in detail immediately after Foros, after the shock he experienced as a result of the attempted coup and his betrayal by the people closest to him. But being a politician, Mikhail Sergeyevich quickly realized that society had changed radically after the coup. Only two days later he spoke the words quoted at the beginning of this section: "Everything must be changed." But even after the coup he remained a man with his own convictions.

It is easy to judge from the sidelines, but it is always easier to free yourself from old ways of thinking if you have not been very convinced of those ideas, or if you are younger and less involved in the ideology and the system. For my part, I am very surprised by what Gorbachev has done in the way of reinterpreting Soviet history, making people aware of new realities and realizing the prospects. After all, the most difficult obstacle to overcome is the self. Gorbachev often liked to say that we are all children of our time. True, he showed himself to be a son of his time, but he also turned out to be capable of carrying out changes and transformations which were incredible for a man of his experience.

I beg the reader to ponder once again the various thoughts quoted at the beginning of this chapter. Without such analysis of the roads and crossroads of philosophy, Perestroika cannot be understood. I have no doubt that these and similar ideas were in Gorbachev's mind. He had an excellent knowledge of history, he read and absorbed the works of the great Russian philosophers (among whom Berdyaev and Fedotov occupy a prominent place) and he read all sorts of material amazing those who saw him "on the job" with the breadth of his interests and his energies. We wondered where he found the time.

I am not saying this to flatter the last president of the USSR. Nobody needs that. I simply wish to relate what I saw and what I know. For example, in the middle of December 1991 a conversation took place between Gorbachev and Mikhail Shemyakin, a well-known Russian artist living in the United States. He flew in to meet the president on the eve of his visit to Pakistan, where he was to deal with the question of Soviet soldiers taken prisoner in Afghanistan. For several years Shemyakin has been making great efforts to liberate his countrymen from prison. This was not his first meeting with Gorbachev, so much of what they said continued from earlier

The Russian painter Mikhail Shemyakin, who lives in the United States, facing President Gorbachev in the Kremlin. Gorbachev is accompanied by the Deputy Foreign Secretary W. Petrowski and Vladimir Yegorov (with glasses).

conversations. The President and the artist spoke first about the problems of the prisoners. Then Shemyakin asked to hear about the changes taking place in the Soviet Union; he was especially concerned about the problem of relations between the peoples.

At one point in the conversation there was a pause when they came to discuss whether the escalating tensions might lead to catastrophe. I interjected that if we followed the ideas of L. N. Gumilev, the Russian nation would have every chance of a real revival, through "ethnic regeneration," which would enable us to cross all the obstacles ahead. Mikhail Sergeyevich immediately began to talk about the great impression made on him by this profound and original scholar's book, *The Geography of Ethnos in a Historic Period*. He spoke about the theory of ethnogenesis as if that branch of knowledge were familiar to him professionally and of interest to him. I am not sure that one could have found many other politicians or statesmen at the time who would have found a need to study such scholarly problems. I think such examples are instructive.

To complete my reflections on the philosophy of Perestroika, I want to stress the following: Somewhere between 1987 and 1988, the ideology of reform began developing a set of contradictions which exploded the theory of Perestroika from within—the contradictions of proclaiming both reform and revolution at the same time. People carrying out reforms do not attack the foundations of a regime, while revolutionaries destroy such foundations. Gorbachev, leader and initiator of Perestroika, was unable to extract himself from the grip of this dilemma when he still had the power to determine policy and direct the processes of transformation. After the coup, when he finally decided to set himself apart from all the basic attributes of the neo-Stalinist model of society, the country had already developed beyond him—if not on its own, then through Gorbachev.

Many of our philosophers, historians and political scientists did analyze these problems and make wise prognoses. But other forces in Gorbachev's team were influencing his thinking, and Gorbachev himself was always so independent that he simply rejected views that did not appeal to him. You would write a note and pass it to the President, and there would be no reaction. We often talked about this among ourselves, somewhat surprised. At the beginning I thought that this behavior did not extend to his closest advisers, but it seems it did, since Aleksandr Yakovlev speaks of it in interviews.

We spoke of this problem at the Free Speech club in May 1991 in a discussion of the question, "April 1985–April 1991— What Happened?" On that occasion the philosopher Guseinov said (quoting from a recording):

> [Perestroika] revealed the fact that tucked away in the depths of the Soviet system there are new forms of social behavior, and they reflect its characteristic features as if in a concave mirror. . . . The illegal ideology is

permeated with a good share of cynicism and verbosity, the shadow economy is very much like the Mafia, the longing for western values looks like external imitation, and the dissident movement is replaced by simple rejection. And all this has leaked out to the surface, revealing to a considerable degree its lack of vitality.

The forces that have come out of the underground have shown that people do not want to live any longer as they lived before. But they did not, unfortunately, form the beginning of new ways of life; they did not open the path along which we might in the foreseeable future have joined the company of economically prosperous and democratically organized countries.

Consequently, if you take in the slightest degree seriously the declared aim of renewing socialism qualitatively and correcting the deformations of the past, then Perestroika has not taken place. In general it has to be noted that the attempt to correct the 'errors' of our ancestors . . . is a hopeless and fairly stupid business. Living beings who are concerned with correcting the 'errors' of the dead are themselves dead. They are simply rogues who pretend to make changes while in fact changing nothing in essence. History is written at once, afresh. People do not reconstruct buildings built by others; they either use them or build new ones.

I will not argue about the exact epithets used, but I am essentially in agreement with this severe judgment. It was pronounced in the spring of 1991, and it was completely confirmed by autumn.

# 5

# Gorbachev and Public History

It is always possible to detect in an increase of historical inquiry the sign of an awakening need on the part of society to adjust to a new situation that has been created without its help or with its very slight participation, and that awakening bears witness in its turn to the fact that the new situation is already sufficiently established and evident for its consequences to be felt. Public awareness differs from personal awareness in that the latter usually moves from established causes to possible consequences, while the former is disposed to arrive at the causes it seeks from the given consequences. — V. O. Klyuchevsky, *Russian Historiography 1861–1893*.[1]

On the whole I consider that what you are now doing has no precedent in modern history. A huge country with a great civilization but also with deeply rooted authoritarian traditions is trying to change its political system in a peaceful way. I know of no other example. You have undertaken something like Columbus's first journey to America. Perestroika is a sort of journey in search of the new and the unknown, without having an accurate map. . . . I have no intention of repeating what was said by one of the speakers at the 19th party conference who compared Perestroika with an airplane that had taken off but did not know where to land. No. I only want to say that your plan does not have any obvious model that it might follow. You have chosen your own road. And the most interesting thing is that, if Perestroika turned out to be successful, perhaps a new and previously unknown form of democracy would be created. — S. Cohen, interview, in the magazine *Kommunist*.[2]

'Valentin Grigorevich, troubled times have come upon us, terrible things are happening in the Caucasus, relations with the Baltic states are strained. There is unrest in Moldavia, and all this against the background of empty shelves in the shops. Many people have lost confidence in tomorrow. For what sins are we paying so dearly today?'

'For what sins? For having humiliated our own people. For having torn it away from its centuries-long task—constructive labor on the land—because we dragged politics into everything it did, and were governed primarily by slogans and not common sense. For having spoken too many words about internationalism and friendship without noticing the real national problems and quarrels. . . . On the whole there is a sufficient number of sins which are intertwined and tied together in one living lump. A growling, aggressive lump.

'We used to spit on the past as it had been until 1917, and now we are smearing dirt over what came after. You can't build anything good, including 'socialism with a human face,' on just being nasty and rejecting everything. . . . Is it not time to stop pouring filth over the past and to get on with some constructive work?'—V. Rasputin, interview, in the magazine *Dialog*.[3]

Western sovietology and official Soviet scholarship differ from each other substantially in the way they describe and evaluate what has taken place in Soviet history. . . . But they are founded on a common premise: that the October Revolution of 1917 which brought Lenin and his fellow Bolsheviks to power marked a complete break with the previous period of Russian history. . . . For many years now I have been declaring my disagreement with this point of view. I consider that after 1917 there took place in Russia a return to the past and that what came about under Lenin and Stalin was a kind of neo-Tsarism, even though it called itself 'socialism.' In the light of this I suppose that the latest developments in the Soviet Union cannot be understood in any real depth without taking the whole of Russian history into account.—R. Tucker, "What Time Is It by the Clock of Russian History?"[4]

The most important peculiarity of Gorbachev's 'revolution' is the fact that it is being carried out by party officials who have faithfully served the previous general secretaries. Times have changed, and so they have begun to preach new views. The Gospel story of the transformation of Saul into Saint Paul has acquired great popularity among them. Legions of Sauls boldly marching to communism made a quick about-turn together, and set off in the new direction as legions of Pauls.

If we compare what Alexander Yakovlev said before the miraculous transformation with what he wrote afterwards it sometimes gives the impression of being a self-caricature. . . . A man who had always hated the

West, above all the USA, citadel of imperialism, who has spent a quarter of a century attacking bourgeois ideology in books and articles in the pious belief that 'the system of private ownership is the cause of the division of society into antagonistic classes,' he now declares, 'In essence the ultimate aim of the class struggle is in peace and harmony.' The world in which, from October 1917 . . . a fierce war was being waged by the new world, fated by scientific laws to be victorious, against the old world, doomed by those same laws to perish, suddenly became 'one world.'

The integrity of the world, our 'common home,' harmony—these became the new slogans of Soviet ideology put together under Alexander Yakovlev's direction, out of bricks preserved and, apparently, forgotten in his store.—M. Heller, *The Seventh Secretary*.[5]

To turn such a huge country around is not a simple thing. There is much to change and clear away, but not down to the foundations.—M. S. Gorbachev, April 1990.[6]

Questions of history are paramount among the problems which determined both the form of Perestroika and, ultimately, its results. Klyuchevsky, the great historian of Russia, pinpointed the principal differences between the developments of personal and collective knowledge: The individual starts by establishing the causes of a situation and then guesses about the consequences. The masses, however, start from their own interests, personal experiences and observations about the advantages or costs of a situation, then turn back to the past and judge history. And in the case of Perestroika, the principal issue, or at least the most important one, over which millions of people disagreed with Gorbachev was his assessment of the Soviet period.

Of course, it would be naive to imagine that people's attitude to Perestroika was more influenced by their attitude to history than by its practical results and above all by the state of the country's economy and by the state of relations between the various peoples. But here is an interesting point: the overwhelming majority of the citizens of the former Soviet Union do not think in terms of a return to the old ways, yet at the same time most do not accept Perestroika. This is borne out by election and referendum results as well as sociological surveys—not only at present or since the August coup, but back to at least the middle of 1990.

Sociologists attached to the Central Committee of the CPSU conducted a survey in November 1990 which showed considerable changes in public opinion. Only nine percent of the people interviewed believed unconditionally in the success of Perestroika; 20 percent counted on success, but with some doubts; and 52 percent reckoned that Perestroika was at a dead end.

"Pessimistic views about the progress of Perestroika are due," the sociologists stated,

> to the fact that people do not see any political force capable of leading the country out of the present chaos. Tired of not having a strong leadership, of economic disorders and other misfortunes, they have recently been losing faith in the constructive role of the party and the soviets. . . . 88 percent of the people interviewed pointed to the absence and steady reduction in the authority of the party organizations of the Communists, and 73 percent made the same point about the declining prestige of the soviets.[7]

Now, these developments must be interpreted in light of Gorbachev's constant defence of the "fundamental values" of Perestroika, including loyalty to post-revolutionary history and the socialist road, faith in the ability of the Communist party to reform itself and to play a new role in a society through the process of reform and democracy, insistence on the power of the soviets, and so forth. In spite of this background, criticisms directed at the General Secretary from party platforms were always described as attacks by the conservatives. In some cases it was true. Indeed, in some cases it led to dramatic situations like Gorbachev's threat to resign at the Plenum of his party in April 1991. But over many problems, the radicals "lashed out" at Perestroika almost as much as the Communists. Some people would not accept Perestroika because they regarded it as a betrayal of socialism, but others saw it as a survival from socialism.

This state of affairs was assessed quite soberly by both the Communists and the Democrats. The Democrats confirmed this by their orientation and policy, while the majority of the people supported them at the time of the coup and support them now (at the beginning of 1992) despite the tremendous difficulties people are going through as a result of the start of a radical economic reform and the liberalization of prices. That the Communists knew the people's attitude to Perestroika is clear from the fact that in January 1991, 87 percent of the secretaries of the central committees of the republican and provincial parties asserted that, in carrying out political and ideological work among the people, the very concept of Perestroika had depreciated.[8] The question naturally arises: How did Gorbachev view these problems? How did he react to the tendencies sketched by the sociologists?

Speaking frankly, I always found it difficult to understand the psychology of Gorbachev's reaction to the sociological polls. Having set in motion the processes of reform and proclaimed the primacy of truth and the policy of openness, Gorbachev repeatedly affirmed his support for that course. At the same time, especially at the outset, whenever it was a question of popularity ratings or of public attitudes to central policy, his reaction was often very sharp and simply did not accord with his assurances of flexibility and openness.

In this connection, I remember a conference we held with leading intellectuals and members of the media, and that famously tense moment in that meeting, about which people have often written already—the criticism directed at the newspaper *Argumenty i Fakty* (Arguments and Facts) and what Gorbachev said to its editor: "Comrade Starkov, as a Communist you ought to offer your resignation." Starkov's offence had been to publish the results of an opinion poll which had revealed that, in terms of comparative popularity, Gorbachev occupied a place somewhere in the fifties. There was a lot of talk about the poll not being representative and about faults in the methods used, but the real issue here was

Mikhail Sergeyevich's reaction to unpleasant information. Starkov refused to resign in the end, and I believe that was the first instance of a high-ranking leader of the party or state issuing an order on a specific personnel question that was not carried out.

I took part in eight or nine such meetings. They usually involved the attendance of the whole Politburo. Speeches were made by journalists, writers and artists. There was almost always a dialogue between Gorbachev and the whole hall, while the rest of his colleagues in the leadership kept silent. Between 1987 and 1989, such meetings took place fairly frequently. Whatever anyone says about them today, in those years they were remarkable meetings. Editors-in-chief, writers and artists were literally bursting to attend because the traditions of the past were still strong and people wanted to hear "at first hand" what was going on, "what life was going to be like." I have recently read things written by people who regarded it as a personal insult not to be invited and who now say these gatherings were not important. That is an opportunist assessment. Those were different times.

Unfortunately, after the meeting referred to, it was more than a year later, at the end of November 1990, until the next one was held. And it turned out to be the last. Gorbachev remained President for another year, but there were no more large gatherings with the intellectuals.

In my opinion, Gorbachev accepted what pleased him and rejected categorically what he found unpleasant. Being an intelligent man—and he is that—he could not overcome a sort of narcissistic factor which, as far as I could see, was encouraged by the people closest to him. On three or four occasions I observed how they reacted even more sharply than Gorbachev himself to reports of the current ratings of the General Secretary and President. No authorities or arguments had any effect here. I saw the first reaction of this kind with the publication in the magazine *Dialog* which gave Gorbachev's rating as 20 percent and Yeltsin's as 59, carried out in June 1990. This result was discussed more in the "corridors of power" than data about confidence in Ryzhkov's government, which showed that the percentage of the population that approved the work of the Soviet government varied from one percent in the Irkutsk region to 12 percent in the Saratov region.[9]

But Mikhail Sergeyevich frequently referred to polls which supported his own aspirations and point of view. For example, he quoted polls in meetings and television interviews which showed that the autumn of 1991 saw the beginning of a new mood among the people in favor of keeping the USSR. That was at the time when efforts were being made to put new life into the *Novo-Ogarevo* process, which was torpedoed by the August coup.

So. The leaders began Perestroika under the banners of loyalty to the cause of October 1917. In 1985, it would have been impossible to start in any other way. But time marched on. Society was changing. People's attitudes were also changing — to history and to the results of following the "socialist road." I well remember how painful it was to think about the future as one read letters addressed to Gorbachev, printed in the press as open letters. Old folk who had served the system honestly for many years, hard-working people, wrote many things as they came to know more about the truth of history. Some thanked Gorbachev for his openness. Others just offered their thoughts or criticisms. But ever more frequently, I came across passages, both in letters of thanks and in letters with curses, in which could be detected the following message: the people, who had now matured and shuddered at what they had learned about their past, would not forgive Gorbachev for having revealed the truth. It was too frightful, too unexpected — simply too shocking.

People can react in a variety of ways to such revelations. The revelations themselves were a victory for democratization and openness, a victory for Gorbachev. But they were also his great tragedy, and it seems to me that this has never been fully recognized. Through his revelations, Gorbachev had linked himself permanently with the past, while the people were moving onwards.

As I write this, I recall congratulating Mikhail Sergeyevich on his sixtieth birthday on March 2, 1991, in good company but without familiarity. (I had not attended other such events.) Afterwards, I glanced through a book I had bought recently — *Thoughts of Wise People For Everyday Use*, compiled in his day by Lev Tolstoy. I opened the page for March 2, but found nothing noteworthy or having anything in common with my ideas of my "boss." But then I opened the page for December 26 — the day my compatriots heard Gorbachev speak for the last time as President. I opened the page and was amazed by the associations that it produced.

Tolstoy gives two quotations: "But Jesus said to him: no one who having put his hand to the plough, looks behind him, is to be trusted in God's Kingdom" (Luke, IX, 62) and "True virtue never looks back at its shadow, but at its good name" (Goethe).[10]

Now, I do not believe in mysticism. But why then was there nothing of any great significance on his birthday, but on his last day as President. . . . Perhaps I did not choose the correct reference point. Instead of his birthday, perhaps we should take his first day in power, the date of his election as General Secretary.

I open Tolstoy's collection of sayings and read what is written for March 11: "God gave His spirit, His love and His reason so that He might be served; but we use that spirit to serve ourselves — we use an axe to sharpen a bigger axe."[11]

Judging by the initials that follow these words — "L. T." — they belong to Lev Tolstoy himself.

You cannot encourage a people to carry out great transformations by trampling their past in the mud. A negative attitude to history is more likely to encourage a destructive or indifferent attitude to present events. So it must be said that the leaders of

Perestroika in the Soviet Union found themselves in an extremely touchy situation. The people had to be told the truth, the whole truth, about the distant and not-so-distant past. Without this, there could be no advances. But the myths and falsifications of Soviet history had entered so deeply into the national psyche that genuine reinterpretation contained some serious dangers for the people's spirits.

This had nothing to do with peculiarities of the Russian character, with nationalism or chauvinism. Feelings of patriotism are an international phenomenon, common to the whole of humanity. Without such feelings it is impossible for any people to have a normal existence. The peoples of the USSR are not the only ones with tragedy in their pasts, but according to the data available, up to four-fifths of the populations of the US, Federal Germany, France, Italy and Spain see their respective country's principal merit as its "past, culture and history." For the people, these values count for more than the level achieved in economic, technological, state and social development.[12] But in recent years we in the (former) Soviet Union have been urged to return to the bosom of world civilization in terms mainly of economic, scientific and legal achievements, forgetting about the cultural and historical foundations of our civilization.

Criticism of the ideology and practice of Stalinism, and in general the frank revelation of all aspects of our country's post-revolutionary history, has often concentrated, not on critiques of the system of the state and its ideology, but on the denigration of history as such and the humiliation of the people as its creator and repository. People felt they were being told of the eternal servility of Russians and the ever-present Russian preference for totalitarian state systems, imperial aims, and so forth. In the long run, the new readings of history certainly did not follow such paths, but in the first years of glasnost, that was where the stress was laid. Western scholars such as Robert Tucker and Stephen Cohen have dropped the masochism of our homegrown historians—many of whom had, before Perestroika, in the main sung the praises of the Soviet decades—

and substituted a style which combines respect and tact with frank honesty.

There has quite recently been an attempt to draw parallels between the histories of various countries and to show that things are not so simple, that all revolutions are tragedies and that the Russian revolution is not an exception but a confirmation of the rule, if we compare it with, say, the French Revolution or the revolutions in England. As well, people have pointed out that not only prosperous America and Germany but the far less wealthy India and China are civilizations, ancient and unique, and so we must not talk about "a return to the world civilization" without asking which "world" we would return to and whether that direction corresponds with our history and our cultural and national mentality.

All such questions and thoughts were immediately branded as conservative and anti-Perestroika. What's more, those labels have had their effects in keeping us down, because the memory is still too fresh of what it means to be branded an "enemy of the people." These are the terrifying remnants of Stalinism.

The contradictions involved in ridding our history of distortions became evident in the aftermath. On one hand, people's minds were cleared of myths and prejudices. On the other hand, this process took place against a background of ever-increasing instability and a worsening economic situation. As a consequence, people began to lose faith in socialist ideas and feel a growing level of alarm, a lack of confidence in the future and a readiness to trust in separatist and nationalist forces which preached that the problems could be resolved better outside the USSR, free from "the center"—which had become the scapegoat for absolutely everything.

Did the people in the leadership see the changes taking place in the minds of the populace? Of course they did. But the people's attachment to the socialist road was always overestimated, right up to the last minute. Sociologists have recently kept repeating that a negative view of the Russian

Revolution and of the Soviet period of our history is increasingly evident. In 1990 more than half the people interviewed had a negative view of the significance of the Russian revolution. Of the people interviewed, 26 percent considered that the revolution was the result of a spontaneous combination of circumstances, 10 percent that it was a coup d'état carried out by a handful of intellectuals and 7 percent that it was a Bolshevik plot.[13]

These changes were particularly potent among youth. In the opinion of 59 percent of pensioners interviewed, "October opened a new era in the history of mankind—the era of socialism." But only 28 percent of students were of the same opinion. Taken together, every fifth young person saw the October Revolution as the moment of the country's entry into a dead end. Among students, 34 percent were of that opinion, whereas among pensioners the figure was 16 percent.[14] As for the historical figures who had contributed most to the country's post-revolutionary period, the first place in 1989, in the opinion of 60 percent of the people interviewed, went to Lenin. At that time age differences had practically no effect on the opinions. In 1990 the older people remained in essentially the same position, but among the young people nearly half of them had changed their view of Lenin's work. If one took only the students, Lenin as an historical figure evoked the admiration of only 38 percent.

A sort of summary of the situation is given in the following figures: In 1987, 93 percent of the people interviewed professed a feeling of pride in their homeland. In 1988, the figure was 63 percent, and in 1990 it was 53 percent. In that same year, when age was taken into account, 76 percent of the elderly were proud of their country, compared to only 42 percent of the young people.

At the same time, there was a notable increase in figures indicating support for national traditions, national culture and the values of the pre-revolutionary history of Russia. This is confirmed by reference to an increased interest in folklore, an increasingly positive assessment of the work of lay and religious figures in science and culture and a practically unanimous consensus regarding the restoration of the historical names of regions, cities and streets.

Thus, a steadily growing majority of the population, especially middle-aged and young people, were seriously reinterpreting their history, starting in 1987. Under such conditions, politicians who involved themselves too closely with history were doomed to eventual defeat.

Before I conclude this section, I must emphasize that great work has been done to rid our historical writings of distortions and restore to the people the truth about their painful history. It was all done on the initiative of the people who started Perestroika. Take the work of the Commission of the Politburo which studied materials connected with political violence and the use of force, headed by A. N. Yakovlev. In August 1990, Mikhail Gorbachev signed two decrees, one restoring the rights of people who were forcibly repressed from the 1920s to the 1950s, and the other concerning the repeal of past decisions by which people were deprived of their citizenship for dissidence. Archives have been opened to inspection and much of the banned literature has been released from the warehouses where for decades even scholars had limited access to it.

Nevertheless, there were questions about which no decisions were taken at the top political level, even problems at the very center of the intellectual and ideological battle. Many of them were quite obvious. There were, for example, matters connected with the restoration of original names to cities, streets and squares. Gorbachev understood very well the necessity for such a move. He approved of the approaches proposed by experts when I handed them to him in the summer of 1990. But the initiative was seized by the local authorities, in places where representatives of the new movements and parties had won elections and were displaying more and more opposition to the center and the President.

It would be wrong to say the official interpretations of Soviet history have not changed. They have changed very substantially. It would be wrong to assert that Gorbachev himself has retained his old view of history. Of course not. But the changes in popular opinion—completely in accordance with the law formulated by Klyuchevsky—were prompted by the decline in the standard of living, the diminished benefits the people received from what the leaders called "socialism." These changes came about much more quickly than a mature and honest politician could change his views, and with all his capacity for compromise Gorbachev was not an opportunist. He believed you could retain your convictions while taking account of political realities. Eventually, he reconciled his historical sympathies with his understanding of political imperatives, but that was already after the August coup and it was already too late.

Ultimately the people and Gorbachev arrived at different assessments of socialism and the October Revolution. This gap was one of the most important reasons for Gorbachev's tragedy.

# 6

# Evolution, Revolutionary Evolution, Revolution

People, people... that is what is most important. People are worth more even than money. You can't buy people on any market or for any money, because they are not to be bought or sold, and it takes ages for them to be formed, and an age means time, some twenty-five or thirty years, even in Russia where the ages have long ago ceased to be worth much. A person of independent thought, active on his own behalf, is formed only by the long and independent life of the nation, through centuries of oppressive labor—in a word, is the product of his country's whole historical life. But our historical life for the last two centuries has not been so very independent. It is quite impossible to speed up artificially the necessary and constant historical factors in the life of a people.—F. M. Dostoevsky, *A Writer's Diary*, 1873.[1]

People who boast that they have brought about a revolution have always discovered the next day that they didn't know what they were doing and that the revolution they have carried out is not at all like the one they wanted to bring about. That is what Hegel called the irony of history, an irony that few historical figures have managed to avoid. —F. Engels, letter, April 23, 1885.[2]

I have very little faith in the ability of the masses to evaluate particular people or particular facts, and in a revolutionary period, when you get a state of mass imbalance, a sort of mass psychosis, that ability is lost completely.... The saying, 'The judgment of the people is God's judgment' is essentially wrong and may well be something inherited from the most distant times of which no trace has been left.—S. I. Shidlovsky, "Reminiscences."[3]

We did not realize, of course, how far we would have to go and what deep changes would be required. This was the cause of our mistakes: In some cases we failed to synchronize our decision-taking, in others we were too late or we were in too great a hurry, didn't think things through, or we destroyed old ways and structures without having created new arrangements.

But it was necessary in practice to get involved in new business, to acquire experience, to get to know more profoundly our society as it was after 70 years of an emergency regime and of isolation from the world, and to learn to take into account the whole of its specific character. It was only then that we came to the final conviction that Perestroika was not to be measured by the usual criteria and nor could it be brought about finally on the principles of the prevailing ideology. . . . The system itself needed changing, the economic and political system needed replacing, the whole multinational state needed reforming in every respect—a real revolution that was called for by the whole of our past and by worldwide progress. —M. S. Gorbachev, *The August Coup*.[4]

[There] is always a chance that, in carrying through Perestroika, Gorbachev will not be able to carry out an economic reform but will cause the Soviet Union to slide into weaker military and political positions. At the same time, if he prefers a safer second alternative, he will have to abandon his plan for major economic improvements in the USSR. He will also have to take upon himself the risk that military technology will develop too quickly for the Soviet Union to keep up with it. Neither the first nor the second alternative appears to be very attractive . . . but the chances are that, bearing in mind the opposition that his reforms encounter and the risk connected with the present radical reform, he will choose the more conservative approach.

In the end, Mikhail Gorbachev, like his predecessors, will in all probability prefer an economy that will depend more on our rich natural resources than on the creative potential of the people. —Marshall Goldman, *Gorbachev's Challenge*.[5]

When we deal with the historical and political research on Perestroika, we always have to bear in mind what I would term "the forecasting of the past effect," or what people colloquially call "being wise after the event." In the end it will be easier to understand why politicians acted as they did if we study the processes of Perestroika itself from the perspective of its own time.

The renewal and transformation of Soviet society was described initially by Gorbachev and most of his allies as reform, then as radical reform and, finally, as a revolution. Gradually, this last definition squeezed out the others, even among those who did not like terminological acrobatics. The talk was not about evolutionary changes but about revolutionary ones. But in practice, right up to the events that followed the August coup, there were no grounds for talking about a revolution. Apart from one episode, which I will discuss, there was not a single change in any sphere of social or economic life large enough to be likened to a revolution. At best, the reforms built up to a critical mass for the transition from quantitative changes to qualitative ones. My opinion in this matter does not accord with the prevailing assessments of Perestroika, but I believe it is true. In fact, it seems to me that a more paradoxical and unusual term—"revolutionary evolution"—is much more accurate.

The first time I came across such a description of Perestroika was in an interview that A. N. Yakovlev gave to the weekly *Sobesednik* at the beginning of 1990. One of the best known leaders of Perestroika, Yakovlev is often called the "generator of ideas," as he played a large part in formulating Gorbachev's own public statements. In this interview, Yakovlev emphasized his dislike for revolutionary shocks. He spoke in favor of profound and substantial changes, but through a gradual process of radicalization—revolutionary evolution.

I think it is politically important to ask, then, who was the first to describe Perestroika as a revolution? Was it a propagandist—seeking ideological insurance through definitions and slogans—or was it from the top, carefully concealed until the right moment arrived? If it was simply a romantic exaggeration of the significance and depth of the policy, then it is understandable why they spoke of revolution when in practice there was too little spirit and force for anything more than moderate reform. On the other hand, if the people who created the policies realized they could not switch immediately to radical measures but had to prepare people's minds for more far-reaching changes, then they were acting either as prophets or two-faced people who talked about sincerity and openness while at the same time conducting affairs behind the scenes.

Future historians will find the answers to such riddles, and the truth was probably more complicated, with each of these scenarios intertwined. Nevertheless, it is clear today that "at the top" there was a thirst for rapid transformation, either through accelerated reform or by a revolution from above. Ultimately, the process turned out to have a will of its own, to live according to its own laws and not by directives or slogans.

I did not determine policy, but I observed in many different situations how policy on the grand scale was made. We often say politics is a dirty game, but I don't believe politicians are especially corrupt by nature. All sorts of people engage in politics. Rather, the question is whether the laws and interests of politics are compatible with moral principles. And it's not just politics. The same can be said of the business world, or of journalism. Yet the old joke that journalism is "the second-oldest profession" doesn't mean all journalists are evil and that all newspapers ought to be closed down.

One of our best-known journalists, my friend Edward Sagalayev, commented in the magazine *Ogonyok* that Gorbachev was amazingly frank, even in his lack of frankness. I was one of the president's assistants when I read this interview, so naturally the words left a trace. But I can recall quite a few occasions when Mikhail Sergeyevich's public speeches—what he said and the way it was received—confirmed Sagalayev's complex but certainly critical verdict. Of course, I also remember many more episodes when Gorbachev's frankness was without any hidden meanings or reservations. And I cannot think of a single meeting or conversation face-to-face with Gorbachev when, even in the face of the most unexpected changes of opinion, he did not explain—or at least give me to understand by a phrase or a gesture—what his attitude was.

I will not say I was always satisfied. Sometimes Gorbachev's "explanations" amounted to no more than "just take it from me" or "there's a lot you don't know, but this is the way it is." But I grew to understand, or at least to trust in the necessity of this as part of the openness and, if you like, the honesty and sincerity of our relations. I never left those meetings with a heavy heart, though certainly I did not always get what I wanted.

Yakovlev once said, in the same interview I mentioned earlier, "Gorbachev is too complex a figure for anybody, including myself, who, I suppose, knows him well, to be able to say for sure what he is thinking at any given moment."[6]

I return again to the questions I started with—who was the first to revolutionize reforms in the Soviet Union? Was it revolution or Perestroika? Perhaps the revolution began and ended with the end of Perestroika?

Let us consider the opinions of two very different people. First, the legendary woman revolutionary, one of the first Russian socialists, Vera Ivanovna Zasulich. She remained to the end a supporter of social-democracy and actively followed the left-radical Communist line in October 1917. Zasulich wrote these lines as part of an argument with N. A. Dobrolyubov and his article "Russia on the Eve of the Twentieth Century," but when you read them today, it is almost as if the article had been called "Russia on the Eve of the Twenty-First Century."

"In Russia," Zasulich wrote,

which for two centuries the government itself has pulled to and fro, where reforms and counter-reforms . . . follow one after the other and without a halt, where the country's whole economic system is undergoing an intensive process of transformation, where, for two centuries already, all the ideas developed by European civilization come down to us from above . . . in such a country, so that no one should upset the government, it is not sufficient for people 'to kill in themselves their thoughts and will and moral dignity'—that is being done on a vast scale. What is needed is that there should be nothing left for them to kill.⁷

The second quotation is from a Spring, 1991 interview with Richard Pipes, director of the Russian research center at Harvard University. His view seems to me to be noteworthy as an expert assessment in the discussions about Perestroika, as reform or revolution, and about which way we were intending to go in those years under Gorbachev and where we are going now:

> There are in socialism fundamental defects that make it impracticable and unpopular. It is a doctrine of intellectuals. Socialism has never been a doctrine of the masses. The masses have never been socialist; they are in principle very conservative. And socialism was imposed . . . by force.
>
> You want to acquire the best that the West has. . . . But I simply do not believe that these two systems are compatible. I like to tell the following story. When Gorbachev visited Britain in 1985 or 1986 he saw that there was a left-wing movement there. He made contact with many English people, and the ancient English civilization and the civilized ways of the English made a great impression on him. So when he returned to Moscow he announced at a meeting of the Politburo that he thought it desirable for Russian traffic to switch to driving on the left side of the road. His proposal evoked a lot of protests and after a stormy debate the Politburo arrived at a compromise solution: half the transport would use the right-hand side of the road and the other half the left-hand side. That is what, in simplified form, a mixture of the two systems would look like.⁸

For a long time, and to some extent for centuries, as Vera Zasulich writes, a situation existed in our country that enabled the authorities to impose practically anything on society and its citizens. And after the revolution, with the dictatorship of the proletariat, they could impose *absolutely* anything. As a result, they trampled down the aspirations and dignity of the people and destroyed those millions who did not conform to the doctrines of the regime.

The communist theory of social change fitted well with this form of power. As a product of the intellectual mind, as Pipes formulates it, socialism came to determine every aspect of life in our society. But it must be said, in the first place, that it was a very specific, Stalinist socialism. As well, the conservative attitude of the public which Pipes describes does not appear only when socialism is imposed on it from above. You might even say conservatism on the everyday level is essentially free of ideology—it also arises when anti-socialism is imposed from above.

Stalin came into conflict with conservatism of the first kind, despite all his talk of the Russian people's love for communal life, collectivism and, consequently, socialism itself. Gorbachev came up against conservatism of the second kind, since decades of life under Stalinist and neo-Stalinist regimes could not pass without some effect. Stalin went in for mass repression. Gorbachev wanted to bring about revolutionary changes by peaceful means, constantly reinsuring himself wherever there was likely to be a break with traditions and people's usual lifestyles. Gorbachev's style of thinking can perhaps be compared to the way revolutionaries think. But there is no evidence that his political behavior differed from the way reformers behave. For this reason, in my view, he was able to carry out a revolution in only one "sphere"—in people's minds. Even there, he was able to change their ideas, but not so much their basic psychology, which is in principle more resistant to persuasion.

I recall being impressed by the dissatisfaction of many journalists and writers, after that last meeting with the intelligentsia, over Gorbachev's insistence on the unalterable attachment of our cooperative and state farm workers ("peasants") to the collective forms of managing the economy. They will not go for the private ownership of land, he would say heatedly, referring in detail to the life his grandfather led as an organizer of the collective farm movement, and to his father's and his own experience of farming. (Gorbachev often backed up his arguments with examples from his own life.) The writer Boris Mozhayev, a great expert on country life, took issue with him.

I'm sure Gorbachev recognized intellectually that the need to diversify the economy would entail the legalization of private ownership, including the ownership of land. But family and collective psychology exerted a powerful inertial force even on this man. He must have figured that if he found it so difficult to break away from this tradition, the mass of people, too, must have been unready to take such decisive steps—in the case of land reform, a real revolution, not of words but of deeds, which would mean the death of society as it was.

The tragedy and paradox of the Soviet period was that the socialist principles of the revolution had promised to create more equitable relationships in society, establish social justice and liberate humanity's creative forces. It worked out quite differently in practice.

In the economy, throughout the administration and even in the whole philosophy of the state, the "real secret of 'real socialism' exposed by Perestroika consisted in the fact that it served as a verbal cover for a privately owned corporation represented by the party and government *apparat*—the actual owner and disposer of the national wealth."[9] This is the final result of the illusions held by the first Soviet leaders.

In the beginning, Lenin considered that state capitalism along with the dictatorship of the proletariat was actually socialism. His ideas later changed and he decided to introduce the New Economic Policy, which recognized a multistructural economy and left room in it for private property. But it was all brought to an end. Beginning with Stalin, the state gradually became the only property owner. Within this "privately owned corporation," as L. V. Karpinsky described the monster, any principles opposed to private property were in fact totally suppressed, because officials and members of the *apparat* were the real joint owners of all property. They were also joint owners of their positions as officials. It was a way of removing all personal responsibility for property.

So it was no accident when a battle was fought in the Perestroika years between those who wanted a new model of social progress and those who opposed a tough, all-embracing program. Gorbachev was the most prominent and presumably one of the most active supporters of the second point of view. At the same time, it must not be forgotten that practically to the very end of Perestroika, all the advocates of the free and democratic development of society still talked in terms of the reform of socialism.

For a long time in the West, scholars with a good knowledge of the USSR did not consider it possible to bring about radical reform in a revolutionary manner. As an example, read what Marshall Goldman has to say, above, about the desirable but problematic character of any radical Perestroika. Or the following, from the prominent American specialist Thomas Naylor in 1988:

> If Gorbachev wants to succeed he will have to change the system of values of the largest society in the world free of social risk—a society whose distinguishing features are full employment, cheap housing, a free education system and free health service, cheap public transport, the absence of bankruptcy and a socialist way of life. But it is precisely this system of values that he is trying to change, and he is doing it very effectively.[10]

It is legitimate to inquire whether it was wise to reject such social achievements. Would it not have been sufficient to carry out the originally planned policy of speeding up economic and technological progress? Were Yegor Ligachev and Gorbachev's other opponents right? No. A radical reform was essential, and only a failure to understand the basic reasons why the USSR fell behind economically could persuade people otherwise.

The problem with what was called the socialist system, in my opinion, was the exclusion of the creative, intellectual potential of the people. Our society tried to compete with Western, post-industrial societies by employing only the intellectual and creative resources available to the leader and his closest colleagues. It was impossible to research, to experiment or to make mistakes in any field, except to the degree it was approved and predetermined from above.

The deliberate construction and administration of a society

based on a sound theory and fair principles seems an attractive idea. But our experience has shown that such an ideal model cannot be brought to life and made effective, free and humane unless every seat of power is held by intelligent, honest and moral people. But that is an unrealizable dream, a utopia.

So perhaps Perestroika is a revolution after all, if it presupposed a departure into a fundamentally different system in economics, politics and cultural life?

Despite our present critical attitude to Marxism (not so new to the Western reader), that doctrine includes theses and postulates that must not simply be discarded. It is a part of the history and culture of humanity. For example, Marxism holds that every revolution and every major social upheaval is preceded by a revolution in people's minds, a philosophical revolution. I believe that such a revolution took place in Soviet society, although it followed a zigzag course of contradictions. In the minds of the public as a whole there was only one little step needed to dot the last $i$ and prepare for the actual transition to a new order. That "trifle" came in the events surrounding the failed August coup, without prompting from the radical politicians, though not without their participation. In three days, the political balance passed its critical point—a point the public consciousness had passed already, though it had been unstable, swinging from one side to the other.

Perestroika advanced like a revolution in people's minds, but in practice it arrived very slowly at the level of radical reform. For a long time Gorbachev played a leading role in this double-process. As General Secretary and then as President, he fulfilled his mission as an educator—a rough role even in a school, let alone in a society in crisis. Yet Richard Pipes points out that teaching is the duty of the head of state: "As President, Gorbachev is obliged to educate his citizens. In a democratic society the president fulfills a pedagogic function. Presidents educate the people and explain to them what is what."[11] So Mikhail Sergeyevich made a lot of speeches. He frequently repeated the same thing over and over again, trying to reach everyone. Sometimes you had the impression that he alone was carrying the burden of persuading people of the need to change without going to extremes and without confrontation. Quite quickly, the people around him became polarized, and he stood in the middle, defending a centralist policy, taking painful blows from both right and left.

He was well aware of the situation, talked openly about it and sought a way out. I remember, during his first trip into the provinces as president, Gorbachev would think aloud about changing his image and the need to find a different style of communicating and public speaking. But, being a man who was easily carried away, he could not abandon the public image which had done so much so quickly to increase his authority at the beginning of Perestroika.

I believe that Perestroika always remained exactly what it was proclaimed to be at the outset—a revolution from above. However, Boris Yeltsin has offered a different interpretation, and it is important to grasp the meaning of Yeltsin's words. They may reflect too severe a view, but it is the view of Gorbachev's principal political opponent and the leader people turned to when they abandoned Perestroika's creator.

Yeltsin said in December 1990:

> It must be admitted frankly that the Soviet leadership today does not have a precise political course for the country's renewal. At first sight its actions look more like improvization, a failure to react to circumstances as they emerge, and endless maneuvering. But behind them is a stern political logic aimed at destroying the sovereignty of the republics and sabotaging the radical reforms. As a result we have today a central authority of 'national no-confidence.'
> 
> The so-called revolution from above is over. The Kremlin has ceased to be the initiator of the country's renewal or an active guide to what is new. The processes of renewal, having been blocked at the center, have transferred themselves to the republics.[12]

But the idea of "people at the top," referring to a revolution "from above," is in no way a synonym for the concept of the "center" or the "Soviet leadership." The fact is that every republic decided to carry out its own revolution from above. The absence of a "revolutionary command" over Yeltsin did not in any way mean that the revolution from above had come to the end for Russian society and the peoples of Russia.

In the last months before the coup—and primarily with the help of its leader—Gorbachev made great advances in policy. What Gorbachev was now saying, as written in the Summer 1991 draft program of the CPSU, hardly differed from the policies of Western social democracy (as represented, for example, in the "Declaration Concerning the Principles of the Socialist International" adopted in Stockholm in 1989.) Perhaps only the technological trappings remained. But the August coup brought that process to an end.

Subsequent events, more than the coup itself, showed that the public agreed the effort to reform the system through Perestroika, particularly as defended by Gorbachev, had failed. At that point, it wasn't only Perestroika that came to an end. It was the whole period of Russian history which began in 1917.

I am convinced that in the final analysis, whenever that may be, Perestroika will be judged by whether we succeed in avoiding large-scale bloodshed, as in the Yugoslav pattern of "solving" national conflicts. But the truth of the saying "the judgment of the people is God's judgment" becomes apparent only after years, or even decades, have passed. For example, in the public mind the collapse of the old Russia is still associated with October 1917, as the work of the Bolsheviks. But the Bolsheviks would never have emerged from the shadows without the February revolution of 1917. The men of February led the Bolsheviks to power. Similarly, the belief may prevail that if the democrats who have now come to power succeed in carrying through reforms, and life begins to improve, it is to their credit alone. If even more painful ordeals lie ahead, that will be blamed on Perestroika. Yet Perestroika, with all its weaknesses, was working only for the first variant. God preserve us from taking the second way.

As well, even such an unquestionable achievement as, in my view, the revolution in people's minds can be reinterpreted, since we still do not know how thorough this revolution was or how committed and stable the new politicians will be. Politics might yet be decided by neo-Marxist social transformations and neo-Bolshevik deeds. The words quoted from Dostoevsky, Vera Zasulich, and Richard Pipes in this section force us to think about the long life of these problems.

In the third place, as we struggle to decide exactly what Perestroika was, reform or revolution, we must read very carefully Gorbachev's writings about the coup and its consequences. We must understand how he missed the opportunity to carry out a revolution in his own mind—to reject resolutely what he had only yesterday defended and personified—if we want to understand his tragedy as a politician and as a man. Gorbachev's book *The August Coup* is an exceptionally frank account to be written by a leading politician, especially when still in power. It is a very painful book; even my own knowledge of Gorbachev's character is enough to tell me what it cost him to write certain sentences and reveal certain events. Observing the president after reading his book, I kept wondering, What sort of strength must a person have to adapt so completely to a mission in life, such that, practically always and in everything, the politician controlled, directed and supported the man?

I do not want to get immersed in the kind of scholarly discussions we had in Russia during Perestroika, over such problems as "the need or ability of proletarian and socialist revolutions to engage in self-criticism and to reject earlier achievements through a new revolutionary transformation." I simply wish to emphasize that if the following statement by Gorbachev is correct, then Yakovlev was guilty of great understatement in saying no one knows what Gorbachev is "thinking at a given moment":

> What the Congress [the Fifth, and last, extraordinary Congress of People's Deputies of the USSR, September 1991] brought the country was not at all unexpected or contrary to the general direction of Perestroika. On the contrary, there took place an explosive liberation of the whole potential for social, economic and national development which had accumulated in the course of Perestroika and was present from the very beginning of its basic concept.[13]

I don't think it necessary to write in any detail about the fact that the Fifth Congress was a congress of deputies who were depressed and paralyzed. In practice the Congress only tried to give a certain semblance of legality to what already had been done or was being done in the Russian political center — in the Kremlin and in the other republics. The "explosive liberation" of Perestroika did not take place at that congress but earlier, on the streets during the coup and in other republics' parliaments and government buildings. This congress was the last, though quite successful, attempt by the center and by Gorbachev to command the situation again. According to all the documents, resolutions and statements by politicians, including the president himself, the policies of Perestroika included very little of what followed the coup. And if these transformations were indeed "present from the very beginning," they were clear only to Gorbachev and he never spoke about it publicly to anyone.

Perestroika prepared the revolution. But the revolution itself began in the course of resisting the coup. And it is continuing today, not according to the socialist scenario of Perestroika, but according to a scenario which will become clear only with the passage of time. We are a country of prophets now. Every politician and political scientist behaves like an oracle, but I have not the slightest desire to join in this chorus.

There are a lot of scholars and politicians who long ago cast off the old dogmas and ideologies. I do not belong to their circle, alas. But I think I have the right to comment about what does not fit in with the true history of Perestroika, because in an absolute majority of the cases when I had the opportunity, I proposed and defended positions and projects that continued the process of transforming society. I would not be telling the truth if I made myself out to be a radical, but there were such cases. We all took part in the revolution of the mind. Now, as I wrote in my earlier book, I no longer believe in any socialisms or capitalisms. At the end of the twentieth century, civilization is developing political structures that do not fit into such ideological schemes.

I am convinced that any revolution is a tragedy for a people, or at least a very painful ordeal. The need for revolution arises when a regime finds itself unable to solve the accumulated and pressing problems through a process of radical reform. That is what I used to believe, and Perestroika reaffirmed my views. As to why society moved from unrealized reforms to revolution, for objective or subjective reasons, that's another question.

Do we belittle Perestroika by saying it was not really a revolution? I am convinced of the very opposite. Perestroika was such a major turning point, even in the centuries-long history of my country, that it has no need of superficial embellishments. Nor does Mikhail Gorbachev, the person who personifies Perestroika, have need of any exaggerated praise. The Russian philosopher and revolutionary G. V. Plekhanov wrote almost a century ago, in an article entitled "On the Threshold of the Twentieth Century," that "Political freedom will be the first major cultural achievement in Russia in the twentieth century."[14] It has come at the very end of the century, but Perestroika has brought about that freedom.

# 7

# What Happened in the Perestroika Years?

To be disappointed with history, or more precisely to place one's hopes in it and to receive nothing in return, is the constant lot of people on this earth. One might say that hopes are instilled into a person so that, lured by them, he will perform certain deeds that are necessary to bring him into a state that has nothing in common with those hopes but that is very harmonious and clearly necessary in the general sweep of world history. To think that people really make history—that is manifest rubbish; they simply live in it, stumbling around without any clear vision of the whys and wherefores. We can only hope that the stumbling progress is not in vain. —V. V. Rozanov, "Where is the True Source of the 'Battle of the Century'?"[1]

When there is an excess of history a person ceases to be a person, but without an excess of the unhistorical he would never have begun and never have dared to be a human being.—F. Nietzsche.[2]

Oswald Spengler rightly pointed out that in different cultures the very idea of the state is different and that there is no definitive 'best' kind of state to be taken over from one great culture to another. And Montesquieu said that there is a specific form of government for every state according to its size, and that you could not get away without transferring the form without reference to the size of the country.

The thing is, for a given people with its particular geography, historical experience, traditions and psychological make-up, to devise a system that will not lead to its decline but to its prosperity. The organization of the state must unquestionably take into consideration the traditions of the people. —A. I. Solzhenitsyn, "How We Can Reorganize Russia."[3]

The path taken by the West is, after all, the ideal that is worth aspiring to. But . . . [the] Western way of life did not come about yesterday. It is the result of many centuries of history, full of human tragedies, bloody wars and uprisings, the exploitation of other peoples and other phenomena about which we learned in Russia in school but have now forgotten about in this attack of mania for the West. Russia cannot be an exception to the general rule. On the path of Westernization, Russia is more likely to run into a new tragic period as a result of which a negligible minority of by no means its best people will come out on top, while the majority will be cast into an abyss of suffering. —A. A. Zinovyev, *I Want to Tell You About the West*.[4]

The word 'Perestroika' can be heard today in all the languages of the world since the attention of many millions of people is concentrated on the changes taking place in the USSR: after all, upon their outcome depends the fate, not only of world socialism but to a large extent of the whole of mankind. The radical transformation of social relations and the removal from them of distortions and additions alien to socialism is an exceptionally important opportunity for our people. It is essential that we carry out a far-reaching and all-embracing reform that will affect the economic, political and social spheres of life. It can be said with confidence that our society has never hitherto had to grapple with tasks of such difficulty. —T. I. Zaslavskaya, *Perestroika and Socialism*.[5]

The political and economic crisis in our country has reached a dangerous limit. The long, drawn out breakdown of the Communist system is threatening to destroy the very foundations on which society and the population are based. Already condemned but clinging stubbornly to power, totalitarianism, striving to prolong its life, is playing with the lives of millions . . .

The malignant quality of 'real socialism,' the irresponsibility and lack of ability of the ruling party have brought the country to the verge of starvation and poverty. The people have lost hope in any changes for the better. Confidence has been destroyed in the incompetent and dishonest Soviet government and in the parliament and president who are incapable of taking far-reaching and decisive steps. The complete collapse of the state system is approaching. —From the Declaration issued by the Democratic Russia movement, October 1990.[6]

The country is on the eve of acquiring a new structure both as a state and as a society. Political reform has brought us to the point where the state has not only taken on a different form but will also change its name. Society is rapidly freeing itself from ideology. The monopoly of power by one party is being replaced by pluralism. *Glasnost* and freedom of speech have already become an indispensable feature of public life. Economic reform has rendered irreversible the transition to a market economy on the basis of a variety of forms of property. Both these reforms have opened the door for the country to enter the world economic system according to the 'common rules of the game.'

The new thinking has contributed to such changes in the world situation that it has become possible, at least in the principal aspects of security, to pursue a single and in the fullest sense a *global* policy. One rarely hears anyone speak of the threat of a world war. These are the most important and most evident changes on an historical scale after six years of Perestroika.
—M. S. Gorbachev, from an article written in Foros.[7]

If we may elaborate on this summary, which Gorbachev wrote during his holiday in Foros shortly before the August coup, exactly what did happen in the Perestroika years?

Well, we began by trying to update the economic system in the typical way, using the latest developments in technology to bring about rapid economic advance. It did not work. We proceeded with difficulty towards making some enterprises independent and developing the cooperative movement, and made some progress that way. Then, slowly, painfully, after overcoming the thinking habits of seventy years, society came to accept the need in a multistructured economy to liberate the initiative of collectives, associations, cooperatives and private entrepreneurs.

This begs the question: Which was more difficult, changing the people's expectations or wiping out the stereotypes that shackled our politicians and economists? After all, they swore by Lenin, but in fact they moved so slowly towards changing property relations that by 1988 we had still not even fulfilled the economic renewals promised by Lenin's New Economic Policy.[8] Indeed, it seems to me that even in 1991 we have not yet equalled the NEP.

As I write, our economy is experiencing a serious crisis, a decline in production accompanied by the destruction of economic links. The abandonment of the old production incentives and the inefficiency of the new ones have eroded the standard of living and caused discontent. Nevertheless, there is an overwhelming consensus that there is no way back, that the future of our society lies in further radical reforms and the creation of a market economy — an understanding the country has arrived at as a result of Perestroika. Post-Perestroika leaders now have no choice but to follow through.

Why, then, did the people who initiated Perestroika not embark on fundamental economic reforms in the first place, instead of just talking about them?

The first and most important reason was the drive to preserve centralized management of the economy, which left no scope for a full-blooded market. Historians will have to research why that happened and how the mechanism worked to obstruct radical economic reforms. Party conservatism and the machinations of the military-industrial complex alone do not explain it. It seems to me that at the highest levels of power, right up to the beginning or middle of 1991, there was no deep commitment to the switch to market relations. This, despite the fact that the planned economy

> has in every case lost the competition for efficiency with the market economy. At best it was capable, at the cost of tremendous efforts, sacrifices and losses, to mobilize resources for very limited objectives in the industrialization and militarization of the country. This becomes evident in a comparison of the 'two Koreas,' or Maoist China and Taiwan, or the 'model socialist German Democratic Republic' and the Federal German Republic (as became quite clear after their reunification). . . . Finally, although there was a great difference in their post-war positions, there is the rapid advance of Japan compared with the Soviet Union.
>
> No less persuasive are the quantitative statistics for economic and social efficiency. Thus, in 1987 (i.e., before the beginning of any economic reform in our country) the gross national product per capita in the USSR amounted to 2,929 rubles, compared to $18,565 in the USA and $14,790 in Japan. The average life expectancy was respectively 70, 75, and 78 years, and expert assessments of the quality of life did not include us in the first one hundred countries of the world.[9]

Did our leaders and experts know about this? Of course. How then could they delay reform? The second reason was that they feared a social explosion. They were convinced that the population had been "spoiled" during years of socialism by low work expectations and a standard of living which, though not high, was acceptable and more or less the same for everyone. As a result, the leaders thought, the people were not ready for a decisive reformation. If true, this would be a very serious problem. The question should not be neglected.

But let us turn from fantasy to fact. According to a survey made in March 1991, in twenty-two regions of the country, 57 percent of the people questioned were convinced supporters of a vigorous transition to a market economy, while only 28 percent opposed it. Moreover, practically half the people (49 percent) considered the switch to the market an essential, long-term change. An additional 21 percent saw market reforms as a necessary temporary measure.[10] So the majority of the population were for a decisive shift to market relations.

Now, perhaps it was only in 1991 that people arrived at this point. Nevertheless, we must point out that people had pinned their hopes on reforms before, and had been disappointed because the reforms had become bogged down. Professor T. I. Zaslavskaya, whose words are quoted at the beginning of this section, once cited the results of a series of surveys. According to these figures, from 1980 to 1986, in the Alta region for example, the proportion of agro-industrial leaders which supported radical Perestroika rose from 12 to 39 percent. But in the course of Perestroika, in 1987, it dropped to 31 percent. This tendency is confirmed by other opinion surveys. Analogous processes took place among the workers.[11]

Economic reform came slower than the leaders had promised, and a majority of people were more and more dissatisfied with the results, causing the national leadership's authority to crumble. The prime minister, N. I. Ryzhkov, whose functions were identified mainly with economic policy and the introduction of presidential rule, fell into extreme unpopularity. In the summer of 1990, it amounted to 8 or 9 percent in Kiev and Zhitomir, and 1 percent in Leningrad, Gorky, Irkutsk and Kemerovo. And despite the impressive democratic reforms he had to his credit, Gorbachev's standing also declined. His rating in those cities ranged from 21 to 7 percent. At the same time, the principal critic of the government's program, Boris Yeltsin, had a rating in the main centers ranging from 65 to 38 percent.[12]

In 1991, the crisis of confidence in Perestroika worsened, intimating more clearly that both the reform process and the decline of the regime were irreversible. According to data gathered by the All-Union Center for the Study of Public Opinion in November 1990, people were asked, "After Gorbachev took over the leadership in 1985 did your life become better or worse?" Seven percent of the people questioned said their lives had improved, 22 percent said it had made no difference, 14 percent found it difficult to answer, and 57 percent said life had gotten worse.[13]

In December 1990, only 2 or 3 percent of the people questioned were expecting any improvement in the country's economic situation. Further economic difficulties were forecast by 63 percent of the population. People no longer cherished any illusions about how long it might take to emerge from the economic crisis—15 percent said four or five years, 16 percent said until the year 2000, and 32 percent thought it would take much longer. Twelve percent even replied that recovery would *never* come about in our country.

Professor Zaslavskaya writes in this regard:

> [There] is scarcely any point in introducing market relations 'by force' without having persuaded a biased people. But, on the other hand, the state of the economy demands immediate attention. In this connection, the question of what is the real opinion of the majority of the people about the state of the economy and ways of restoring it to health acquires special topicality.
> An analysis of the data gathered showed . . . 70 percent of the people questioned were in favor of setting up enterprises belonging to the employees and rented by them. Sixty-nine percent were in favor of working jointly

with foreign firms, 45 percent favored the issue of shares, 36 percent wanted foreign firms, and 30 percent wanted cooperatives.

People's attitude to private ownership is more complicated. . . . It is true that, to the straight question of what they thought of the possibility of the creation of enterprises belonging to individual citizens, only slightly more than a quarter gave a positive reply, while 40 percent of those questioned disapproved. But in reply to a more concrete question more than three-quarters of the people questioned supported the idea of having private enterprises involved in the treatment of agricultural produce, 73 percent wanted them in trade and everyday services, 60 percent in light industry, and 48 percent in medicine and the school system. Consequently the 'monster' of private ownership turns out on closer examination to be accepted by the population quite calmly.[14]

But a diagnosis of the state of public opinion was not sufficient. The politicians themselves—including those who led Perestroika—had to overcome their own biases. They also had to attract new leaders and specialists to the power structure who would be able to operate in the changed social and economic conditions. Gorbachev's circle did eventually expand this way, but slowly.

One of the most serious social shocks in those years was the strike movement organized by the miners. The situation in the mining industry and in the mining towns was difficult, and remains so. But, significantly, among the delegates elected to the first and second congresses of miners in June and October 1990, 90 percent were supporters of democracy and a market economy.[15] These were the people the working class counted on at that time, the people they elected to represent them. The miners were most active in support of Boris Yeltsin and made severe demands on the governments of both Ryzhkov and Pavlov, which were supported by Gorbachev. Most people definitely associated Yeltsin and his team with a decisive transition to a market economy.

When Yeltsin became President of Russia and then, following the dissolution of the USSR, of the Russian Federation, Yeltsin did initiate radical reforms. One of his first moves was to liberalize prices. Prices shot up, not a few percent, but tens of times. Promised compensation measures were either delayed or inadequate to deal with what was happening on the market. Economists assessed this action mainly as inflation, not liberalization, because in fact the privatization of industry and trade had only just begun and there was no competitive environment. Moreover, only a few months previously Yeltsin had declared April 2 the worst day of his life—the day Pavlov's cabinet had raised prices, to a much smaller extent than Yeltsin would. At that time, he announced that he would never permit an increase in prices.

Clearly, the latitude granted to Yeltsin is much greater than what people allowed to Gorbachev. The Russian president's reserve of confidence has permitted him steps that would never have been taken during Perestroika. From this I can only conclude that democratic reforms are not dependent on economic foundations, which is surprising because during Perestroika we all assumed that in the end everything would be decided by the economy.

At a meeting with the leaders of culture, science and the media in January 1989, Mikhail Gorbachev emphasized that April 1985 had not dropped out of a clear sky. It had been prepared by society, the party and the people. Everything was ready for it. We had serious material prepared. The store of new ideas at that time consisted of some 110 documents and analytical studies that were locked away, as Gorbachev said, in his safe and in Ryzhkov's. Yet at the same meeting, replying to Professor Abalkin, who had criticized the economic program for its lack of thorough preparation and proper discussion, Gorbachev asserted that the "cavalry charge" version of economic reform had not been successful. A "long siege" would be required.

Paradoxes like this betray how and why the economic transformation process ended up in a morass for so many years.

The same motives governed the discussion even in 1991. In March, at a meeting with his advisers and assistants, dealing with the progress of the economic reform, the president said that everybody was asking how long the "center" was going to continue looking at everything so calmly. "You may not understand where everything is going," they said. "The working class might not put up with it. The situation in the main street shops is catastrophic."

Finally, after the coup attempt, I heard Gorbachev tell his immediate circle about his impressions of his trip to Irkutsk and Khirgistan. People understood everything, he said, but there was a limit to their patience. The economic reforms must be advanced decisively. But by then, of course, it would be left to Boris Yeltsin's government to embark on radical economic restructuring in Russia.

When you are an active participant in them, strange events quickly becomes familiar. Social advances come to seem as if they simply stood to reason. It even becomes difficult to believe that a year or two ago there might have been people in our society who would agree to revert to the pre-Perestroika political atmosphere. Yet Perestroika itself started out from small beginnings — at first, simply from the fact that the new Soviet leaders, particularly the new General Secretary of the CPSU, seemed to be capable of thinking and speaking casually with the people. Perhaps the best way to appreciate the scale of all the changes may be to consider how this new style of communication appeared to us only yesterday to be almost a revolution in itself.

Slowly, not without bitter struggles, we left behind the most odious legacy of the authoritarian system, and came to the conclusion that the roots of our social and economic troubles were to be found in political life.

For the first time the country held free elections for people's deputies, with a choice of candidates, with rivalry and competition between candidates and their economic and political programs. From a theoretical recognition of the need for political and ideological pluralism, we arrived at the liquidation of the Communist Party monopoly and an opening for a multi-party system. Presidential government was introduced; legislative and executive bodies were reorganized.

Few people in either the Soviet Union or the West could have imagined two or three years ago that events in our country would develop as they have. Even among those who welcomed Perestroika and applauded Gorbachev's policy, there were many skeptics. The distance we had covered towards democracy and openness seemed too great to be believed. In 1988, for example, the conclusions of the book *The Long Way To Freedom: Russia and Glasnost* were quite typical. The author, Walter Laqueur, chairman of the International Council of the Center for Strategic and International Research, professor at Georgetown University in the United States, and director of the Institute of Contemporary History in Great Britain, says: "There is every reason to suppose that the epoch of Glasnost has reached its zenith and one should not expect further significant advance for a long time. . . . More dramatic and profound changes would amount almost to a miracle, because the cultural revolution is linked not only with the replacement of one political elite by another but also with stable and radical changes in the mental attitude of the whole people. That may come about sometime as a result of a serious shock or as the final stage of many small steps, or after the emergence into society of a new generation. Such a revolution is not, according to all the signs, on the agenda for the present historical stage."[16]

Much of this prognosis has been disproved, though some of it may have come true. The author did not see any prospects for cardinal changes in the USSR in the present historical stage, and certainly nothing like the Union's disappearance. But, on the other hand, he talked about a serious shock as a possible factor to revolutionize the country. Perhaps the attempted coup provided that shock.

The ups and downs of democratization in Soviet society are sufficiently well-known in the West and in Russia. I will not go into them in detail, but I will draw attention to what I regard as some key points.

First, I think the decisive clash between supporters and opponents of Perestroika was the one surrounding an article (March 13, 1988, in *Sovetskaya Rossiya* newspaper) by N. Andreyeva, headed, "I Cannot Abandon My Principles," and the reaction to it in a leading article in *Pravda* (then still the official mouthpiece of the CPSU) on April 5. These matters were later raised on the platform of the 19th conference of the CPSU in June and July.

The essence of Andreyeva's article was that people should not be allowed to reject the conventional interpretation of the Soviet period, including the value of Stalin and his policies, to drag anti-socialist ideas into society "in the guise of Perestroika." *Pravda*'s article firmly rejected this attempt to halt the processes of renewal, saying that Andreyeva's article was essentially a political platform in support of the conservatives.

Patriarch Alexij II visiting President Gorbachev in the Kremlin. Yegorov is to the left of Gorbachev.

The debates that followed in the press and among the intellectuals were stormy and keenly fought. But thanks to these efforts in the press and the decisions of the 19th conference of the CPSU, the way was opened for an extension of the democracy, Glasnost and political pluralism. At that time, to tell the truth, the CPSU's sanction was still required to register and consolidate the victory of a political trend. Nearly everything depended upon the attitude of the General Secretary, Gorbachev, who was firm in his defence of the Perestroika process.

However, around that time, the intellectuals' various professional organizations began to split along ideological lines. Gorbachev tried to hold the writers and the artists together, appealing to them to avoid extremes, but the polarization was too far gone. This was very difficult for Gorbachev, because he sympathized with many artists of the so-called "earthy" persuasion, with their patriotism and concern for their people. But many of the people on this wing of the intelligentsia were, to put it mildly, cautious in their attitude to Perestroika and tended to adopt pro-Russian nationalist views. They moved from a concern with the country's history in general, including the Soviet period, toward a critical attitude to the October revolution and socialism, to which Gorbachev was then unquestionably loyal. On the other hand, some writers and artists who at the outset had been overwhelmingly in favor of Perestroika began to move in a radical-liberal direction and to criticize the October Revolution and socialism from that angle. These attitudes among the intelligentsia were a powerful political factor.

Furthermore, one must distinguish such a "moment of truth" along the path of Perestroika as the reorganization of the administration and the political system—from the radical reformation of the electoral system to the repeal of the clause that made the CPSU the ruling party, Article Six of the Constitution; and from the establishment of a multi-party system to the beginnings of presidential rule. As well, beginning with the first Congress of People's Deputies, in May–June 1990, Russia and its leader Boris Yeltsin began to play an increasingly important part in the country's political life and administration. Yeltsin was elected President of Russia by a substantial majority of voters in June 1991.

This process was certainly difficult, marked by mistakes and inconsistencies, but that does not provide grounds for making one-sided judgments about Perestroika or its results in the political sphere. Nevertheless, there are plenty of such assessments. Here, for example, is what some historians and political scientists have written in a joint work titled *Our Fatherland: An Essay in Political History*:

> In the true sense of the word there never was any Perestroika in the USSR. Gorbachev and his supporters undertook a bold and desperate attempt to revive socialism and to instill new life into a dying system. This is the source of the lack of consistency in his policy, the seeking for compromise and the attempt to combine extensive and palely reformist methods. . . . But, apart from their true aims, the reforms undertaken did a great work. Having demonstrated the impossibility of renewal, they brought about the collapse of totalitarianism.[17]

Or take the conclusion drawn by Mikhail Heller:

> The lie which persuaded people of the possibility of achieving Utopia was what drove the Soviet people and was no less a force than the cruelest repression. Gorbachev allowed people to speak of the existence of the lie. He permitted the introduction into the irrational, mystical Soviet system— founded on the brilliantly simple formula, 'one leader, one party, one people'— elements of rationality, even though they were expressed in the revised vocabulary and in gaps in the lie. A symbiosis of the irrational and the rational is impossible. The organism either rejects the alien body or it perishes.
>
> To the question of why Gorbachev embarked on Perestroika there is only one answer: to delay as long as possible the collapse of the Soviet system.[18]

Much of what is said about Perestroika in these statements is true, both the assumptions and the conclusions. But I must insist that what we had in Russia was both the policy of Perestroika and Perestroika itself. If we are talking about the true sense of the words, then the authors of the joint work quoted above are talking about *novostroika*. And this "new construction" requires us, of course, to approach everything in a different way. But no observer can refuse to respect the sincerity with which people hold their ambitions, whether they are the victors or the losers. This is a moral imperative. After all, the court of history is not a criminal court where people are judged and sentenced. In the courts of history, the main task is to understand. This supreme court also passes judgment, of course, but only on historical criminals, which Gorbachev could be called only by neo-Stalinists and mastodons of dogmatic socialism. In our efforts to be democrats, should we join such company?

Reflecting on the way things appeared in 1988, Thomas Naylor pointed with great foresight to what would be the subject of heated debate in the near future: the problem of Gorbachev and power. He wrote:

> Many sovietologists are of the opinion that, in his efforts to reform the party and the state administration, Gorbachev will be severely restrained by the vast and powerful Soviet bureaucracy. But this point of view seriously underestimates the political power that Soviet leaders have possessed in the course of history. Whatever they say over there, the acceleration of the process of reform under Gorbachev indicates that he has in fact much greater power than one could imagine.[19]

And nobody but Gorbachev has used his power in the name of democratization.

The truth was that in the USSR tremendous possibilities and in effect unlimited power resided with the country's leader, the General Secretary. It remained this way until the CPSU was deprived of its commanding powers and practically the whole state administration collapsed. In fact, nearly the whole state structure fell into ruins, because for decades, ever since Stalin, the CPSU had not been a political party but a state administrative apparatus controlled by politics and ideology. Neither the revived Soviets nor the economic departments of the Council of Ministers had the means of replacing the party at the level of the administration.

The Communist Party of the Soviet Union has not existed since August 1991. But no discussion of Perestroika would be complete without reference to it.

I do not need to tell you that the situation of the CPSU was an anomaly that did not fit in with a state that respected the rule of law, and so on. The question is quite clear and there cannot be two points of view on it if we remain supporters of democracy. Unfortunately, the business of administration does not always operate according to our ideological preferences, and when the CPSU was removed, many important mechanisms of government went along with it.

Nobody has done as much to bring about changes in the CPSU and to alter its status in society as Gorbachev has done. But Gorbachev also understood what the country depended upon, so it was not surprising that there was such a tense battle over Article Six. Nor was it surprising that Gorbachev delayed the solution of that matter with such care and diplomacy.

On June 20, 1989, at the first and last conference of heads and deputy heads of Party organization and ideology, the General Secretary referred to the results of the first congress of people's deputies and said that the same people ought to meet regularly to work out a policy and plan practical action. He based what he had to say on two conclusions: first, the election and the congress itself had shown convincingly that the process of democratization had won the day; but second, the Party had been found to be politically and psychologically unprepared for this, and many had lost their heads and panicked. (That was the first time I had heard such an opinion of the unhealthy situation in the Politburo.)

The General Secretary of the CPSU spoke of the danger of delaying the process of the renewal and democratization of the party itself. The people were right to criticize the CPSU, he emphasized. If we did not overcome the present difficulties we would lose, and the door would open up for anti-socialist forces, he said. He also pointed out that we were for the first time seeing our people not as the object but as the subject of power. The Party was being crushed by its own weight, and the national economy along with it.

To make clear how the leadership at that time understood the processes taking place in society, I must point out that at the Second Congress of People's Deputies at the end of 1989, all the members of the Politburo (Gorbachev, Vorotnikov, Zaikov, Ivashko, Kryuchkov, Ligachev, Maslyukov, Medvedev, Ryzhkov, Slyunkov, Shevardnadze and Yakovlev) voted against the repeal of Article Six. So did all the candidate members of the Politburo and the secretaries of the Central Committee and all heads of department of the Central Committee who were also people's deputies. The only one who voted for the repeal of Article Six was V. M. Falin, head of the international department.

Of course, people who had worked in the old party system remained at all levels of power after the repeal of Article Six. They conducted themselves in various ways. There were whole regions of the country that refused to accept and even sabotaged the reforms. But the CPSU as a force capable of influencing affairs steadily declined.

However, it was not simply by virtue of his attachments and sympathies that Gorbachev held on to the party and the post of General Secretary. He is probably not a consummate pragmatist, but he is no altruist. Once he had become president and had been invested with greater powers, Gorbachev acted like a man and a politician who was well aware of the strength still possessed by the CPSU. Even the structure of the presidential government was based, right up to the summer of 1991, on the structure of the party and was interwoven with it. That was in the higher reaches of the administration, in the contacts between the Kremlin and the Old Square (the buildings that housed the *apparat* of the Central Committee). As far as vertical links were concerned—the links that should have connected the center with the republics and regions—no administrative machinery or structures for presidential rule were created, and Gorbachev remained dependent on Party ties to influence these branches of government. There was talk about correcting this on a couple of occasions, but only indirectly, as far as I am aware.

There are a great many documents to be studied for us to be able to analyze and not just to guess about the relationship between Gorbachev, the CPSU and Perestroika. He wrote in his book following the August coup:

> Casting a retrospective glance back at the events of 19–21 August, I have to say that the logic of the profound reforms did not exclude such a turn of events. I recognized that events could take on extremely dramatic forms. What was the basis for such a supposition? Cardinal changes had affected the whole social organism and the deeply rooted interests of all sections of society. Above all I have in mind the Party, which ruled in the name of the people without obtaining the authority to do so from the people themselves.[20]

Neither I nor any of Gorbachev's other colleagues ever heard him talk about the CPSU in such terms. Gorbachev could not say such things then, if only because of the undesirability of drawing parallels — after all, Yeltsin was elected president by a nationwide vote, while Gorbachev was not. In fact, the General Secretary, who was also the president, was the Party's most powerful instrument, along with the power to appoint officials to government posts, which Gorbachev did, frequently in the face of resistance by the parliament and despite protests by the public.

I write about this only because I believe Gorbachev understood that he had no other support apart from the Party. Opinion polls unrelentingly bore witness to this fact. He did not, of course, cherish any illusions concerning the Party as a community of like-minded persons, and his attitude to other Party officials and their anachronistic thinking became more and more negative over the years. But until the very last day, including the period immediately after the coup and his return to Moscow, he had to rely on the party. I will not dispute that it was possible he felt personal and moral obligations to the party as well. But above all, it was a politician's instinct at work.

When Aleksandr Yakovlev was expelled from the party, not

long before the attempted coup, he said he did not believe it was possible to reform the CPSU, while Gorbachev continued to think it possible. People commented that Yakovlev only said this because of his bitterness over his expulsion. But even back in the spring, after the General Secretary had withdrawn his resignation at the April plenum, I had asked Yakovlev why Gorbachev decided to stay. Surely he did not hope to change the party while still maintaining its unity? Yakovlev replied then, "Gorbachev still believes, but I don't."

Referring to the difficult problems of reforming Soviet society, Gorbachev says quite frankly in his last book: "From the very beginning . . . I tried not to allow an explosive resolution of the contradictions to take place. I wanted to gain time by making tactical moves, so as to allow the democratic process to acquire sufficient stability to ease out the old ways and to strengthen people's attachment to the new values."[21] This process of squeezing out the old by consolidating supporters of the new was until recently part of party policy. In an article written before the coup, Gorbachev said that around the new Party Program, "We must unite all the healthy forces in society who want Perestroika to succeed." And a little further on:

> I will recall once again what I said three years ago — that all of us and the whole party must learn to work in conditions of developing democracy. Everything suggests that the warning was not taken seriously. The party did not keep up with the democratic process in society. And in these conditions there developed an inferiority complex that drove many people into the ranks of the opposition.[22]

It is easy to deliver judgments about these things now, but at that time not much was clear. The authority of the leadership was weak. In the spring of 1991, according to data obtained by the Russian Social and Political Institute, 60 percent of the people questioned in 26 districts of Russia criticized the inability of the leadership of the USSR to stabilize the situation in the country. But, on the other hand, opinions in society concerning Perestroika and democratization were very unstable.²³ It took the coup ordeal to swing the scales over to the democrats.

We often hear that Perestroika achieved its clearest results through Glasnost and its benefits to the national state of mind, which is true. It is difficult to imagine any further advances without a rethinking of our past, without heated and painful debates to overcome dogmatic ideas about civilization and progress, or without the liberation of the creative powers of the intelligentsia and the removal of the extreme restrictions imposed upon the mass media. But the intellectual side of society does not exist in isolation from economics, politics, international relations and cooperation with other countries. Consequently, talk of which comes first, mind before politics or politics before mind, seems rather academic. I am convinced, however, that whatever assessments and reassessments are made in the future they will come to one sure conclusion—that in the Perestroika years society achieved enough self-knowledge to clear space for a future path.

Yegorov with Barbara Bush in the White House.

But when all the praises of Perestroika have been sung, the reader should not be confused by the data quoted about the attitude of Soviet people to democratization. There's no way such a wide spread of opinions and such an unstable balance could have been avoided in the first stages of emancipation, since it was taking place, unfortunately, against a background of a tremendous economic disorders, a catastrophic fall in living standards and an exceptional worsening of inter-ethnic relations. Just put yourself in my compatriots' place, weigh up the situation and do not be too severe or dismissive. All people want to live in freedom, and to be free of worry for their children.

Secondly, a point which in my view was said well in a Soviet TV interview by the Russian-born poet and Nobel prize-winner Joseph Brodsky: that in extreme circumstances people in the Soviet Union behave with restraint and without hysteria. This is a testimony to the nation's maturity. Now, for the first time in my life, I do not feel ashamed of the behavior of the people in whose language I write. Of course, there have been and are in Russia outbreaks of hysteria and extremism. But, after all, democracy does not consist in eradicating non-democrats from society but in ensuring freedom and letting democracy establish itself by democratic means. That, I believe, is the most important and difficult task facing us today.

*"The structure of the state must without fail take account of the traditions of the people."*

These words of Alexander Solzhenitsyn's, in my opinion, reflect the only civilized approach to solving state problems in any country—with the caveat that in a multicultural society, we should speak of "the peoples" instead of "the people." I agree in spirit with the analyses of the author of *Rebuilding Russia*, but I do not subscribe to all his conclusions, which are insensitive to the way particular peoples understand some episodes in our distant and not-so-distant past. Some republics in the former Soviet Union had a very painful reaction to such nuances. However, what matters here is the need to account for the whole complex of historical, cultural, ethnogeographic, and psychological factors that underlie international questions, including the peculiarities in relationships between peoples and states, and the specific ways frontiers and alliances and other problems are framed.

A logical and democratic theory may turn out to be useless in practice if it does not address the whole of this mosaic. An approach might be appropriate in one case but ridiculous in another. Such dilemmas were the submerged rocks in the sea of national-territorial issues that plagued our vast country, which had spread in the course of history to cover a sixth of the world's surface. These "rocks" gave Perestroika its first and sharpest confrontations. They lay at the foundation of the wars of legislation and sovereignty which finally undermined our weak economy and shook the whole structure of statehood.

It was in an attempt to keep themselves away from these "rocks" that the leaders and participants in the August coup emphasized their goal of preserving the Union. These "rocks" were the ones that moved apart and formed an abyss of international misunderstanding, discord and enmity, and then came together again to put an end to both the multinational state and our hopes for a new, open and democratic Union treaty. They also put an end to presidential rule, the rule of the notorious "center." Of course, even if the center had not made so many mistakes on its own initiative, even if there had not been an attempted coup d'état, the country could not have got away without major shocks. And I can see ahead the years and decades it will take for us to sober up and heal the wounds that still bleed. God willing, there will not be fresh ones.

In the matter of the nation-state, Perestroika inherited a troubled legacy, not only from the period before the revolution of 1917 but from the Soviet years, with all their wars and military alliances and conquests and voluntary accession and friendship and interpenetration of cultures and suppression of national identity. What mattered to us was the final outcome: errors and crimes committed against whole peoples so interwoven that, in conditions of democratization, the relations between them could not fail to become the most important issue. Many of these struggles are well-known: Nagorny Karabakh; the secession of Latvia, Lithuania and Estonia from the Union; the republics' demands to be economically independent; and the claims by practically all the non-Russian peoples to be sovereign states. But I want to discuss the period between summer and autumn 1991, when the problem of nationalism in the USSR led the country directly to a new stage, in which the Union practically ceased to exist and the Perestroika policies of Mikhail Gorbachev came to an end at last.

I begin by recalling what the president wrote after debating with the people who saw the resolutions of the 19th conference of the CPSU as "the principal mistake of Perestroika" and "the beginning of the collapse of the party and state." In a book devoted specially to our national problems, A. Avtorkhanov attaches special significance to this conference in the struggle between the reformers and the conservatives, saying, "It is in the interests of the peoples of the USSR that Gorbachev should emerge from this struggle as the victor, but it would be ultimately in the interests of the West if Ligachev should be the victor, because he is as clear in his views as Lenin and as predictable as Stalin."[24] I will not offer an opinion about the West; however, it was not the Politburo but our people who of their own free will voted in the March 1991 referendum in favor of a reformed, freely elected, free and democratic Union of Soviet Socialist Republics with the publication of a new Union Treaty. Those in favor amounted to 76.4 percent of the 80 percent of the population that took part in the referendum.

That was the line that Gorbachev personified. As he put it, "The democratization of society in our country would be doomed if it were not extended to relations between the nationalities and the rights of all peoples." But many of the leaders involved "were either politically inexperienced or simply irresponsible, embittered nationalists" who blamed the "center" for any mishaps because it 'had not taken precautions,' 'not prevented,' 'been too late' or, on the contrary, 'had no right to intervene.' In all these accusations there was only one true message: that the center should have supported somebody's side, and in fact 'my' side, against the other. This is why Gorbachev supported the referendum effort. In the end, as he writes,

> The majority voted in favor of maintaining the integrity of the state, which was a thousand years old and which had been created by the efforts and intellect and by innumerable sacrifices of many generations.... Today a genuinely voluntary community of people is being put together and that will give unprecedented stability to our Union.... The conclusion of the Union Treaty will make it possible at last to stem the destructive processes and make a decisive move towards the restoration of normal conditions of life and work.[25]

Later, Gorbachev comments that "perhaps the most tragic result" of the failed coup was its effect on the "centrifugal tendencies" in the USSR, which suddenly threatened to tear the state apart. "If that were to happen," he says, ". . . all our plans for the future would be just thin air." His formula for uniting the various interests was "that we should create a Union of Sovereign States, on the assumption that that would make it possible to establish a new balance between the centrifugal and the centripedal forces. It was a question of creating a new union state."[26]

As I see it today, though I will have to wait to see if the investigation and trial prove me right, the coup was an attempt to preserve the revived Union, at least within the framework passed in the referendum, but instead it whipped up the centrifugal forces which would lead to a fundamentally new situation afterwards. After the August events, a revolution took place in the country, literally in the space of weeks—a couple of months at maximum. So far, it fortunately has been peaceful, but it bore all the attributes of a revolutionary process. The guidelines of social development changed. Policy was being formed on the basis of different values and ideals. The economy was looking for different kinds of ownership. And, most important, the main question of any revolution was decided—the question of power. Power had really been transferred to new forces, even if it was still personified mainly by the old leaders, for they had practically all changed their political views. Only time will tell how substantial these changes really are.

Even under the most elevated and optimistic appraisals of Perestroika, it has only just begun to deal with a cardinal reform of the state administration. In fact, the national and administrative division of the country—before the collapse of the Novo-Ogarevo process and the proclamation of the Union of Independent States—was until very recently the most stubborn remnant of Bolshevism and Stalinism in the former Soviet Union. The principles and frontiers used in the division of Russia in 1922 were probably among Lenin's biggest mistakes. If he abandoned the utopianism of the first years and adopted different views of socialism—from the point of view of economic development and the relationship between the classes—and if the New Economic Policy drew a line under the previous stage and opened up new prospects for the country, the same cannot be said for his approach to state administration. Lenin deserves the harshest criticism for this, and Stalin later committed even worse mistakes in dealing with the administration.

In essence we have inherited what is for the so-called civilized world a quite unique set of divisions along national, ethnic and geographic lines. We only have to think of the Ulster problem in England or Quebec's position in Canada to realize that even in countries no one accuses of being undemocratic or uncultured, drawing ethnic frontiers within a single country can lead to continual conflicts or even to outright bloodshed. There are dozens of such frontiers in our country. Moreover, as Gorbachev has pointed out more than once, the great majority of them are purely administrative. Only 30 percent of them have the approval of the state; the rest were drawn by local soviets. These internal frontiers of ours frequently have no historical, ethnic, cultural, national or any other logic to justify them. They were never likely to last long, even in the confines of a totalitarian regime, but with the collapse of authoritarian rule the potential energy was transformed into kinetic force.

It is senseless to draw meaningless frontiers. But if it has already been done it is many times more stupid to perpetuate them, to divide the country along the same lines and to break up whole peoples. Seventy percent of the country's internal frontiers, and possibly more, were potential sources of dispute and needed changing. In addition, according to the population statistics, the non-Russian population in Russia amounted to 17.4 percent, the non-Ukrainians in Ukraine to 26.4 percent, the non-Byelorussians in Byelorussia to 20.6 percent, and the corresponding figures for "non-native" groups in other republics were: Kazakhstan, 64 percent; Uzbekistan, 31.3 percent; Azerbaidzhan, 21.9 percent; Khirgistan, 52.1 percent; Tadzhikistan, 41.2 percent; Turkmenistan, 41.2 percent; Moldova, 36 percent.[28]

If we really want to put an end to the cataclysms the former Soviet Union has experienced in the twentieth century, we ought to abolish the national-territorial divisions of 1922 altogether.

"What?" the "democrat" or "national-patriot" will exclaim. "Create the empire all over again?" Of course not. It is not a question of reviewing the frontiers, which would be the quick way to civil war. It is a question of abolishing the frontiers everywhere and banning any further reference to them. Nor would it be an imperialistic trick. We must set the cultural and national autonomy of all peoples, large and small, in place of the thoughtless official divisions and the national-territorial frontiers. Freedom to develop should be granted to nations and peoples and not to territorial formations that are already declining in importance.

We must defend the rights of individuals and peoples and their national identities in every way, and not come to the defense of the political ambitions of national or territorial bureaucrats. They are the ones who are interested in preserving the "republican" divisions and frontiers, to keep a little hay in their nose-bags. Moreover, they are interested in creating independent states only because a local republican leader would then become an instant statesman. The interests of the peoples are to have cultural and national independence, while the interests of the officials and politicians lie in state separatism. That is the crux of the matter.

Does this mean that we have to start all over again as the Russian Empire? Definitely not. That would be stupid. People who call for that today are political speculators not in tune with history. Moreover the "imperial" card is being played both by people who want to return to the period before 1917 and by those who want to receive some dividends by frightening people both in Russia and abroad with specters of Russian imperialism, chauvinism and so on. According to data gathered by the sociologists there are not more than 10 percent of my compatriots wanting to preserve the unitary model of the union state.[29]

As I understand it, the reform of the Soviet federation in the course of Perestroika was an attempt to rid ourselves by peaceful means of a nightmare created in 1922. But the march of sovereignties turned at the outset into a parade of absurdities. People were living in communal, barrack-like dwellings, and they simply privatized the building. But the foundations were the same. The energy supply was still faulty. There was only one water tap and only one lavatory. So they nailed up one door into the corridor and opened up another one. And out the window people went — some to Europe, some to Asia, some to it doesn't matter where, so long as they are outside.

What a house we made. There is nothing here in common with the idea of a common European home or a common Asiatic home, because we set about building it without having thought out its history or ethnic, cultural, national or geographic conditions. The Bolshevik home did not last 70 years. It seems to me that our children will come to curse this new home and will begin jointly to rebuild it. We ourselves may yet change our minds. How many tragedies, and how many losses will it take before common sense returns?

Such questions can and must be decided only on the basis of the law. But the laws have been violated frequently—before, during, or after the Perestroika years. In the course of Perestroika, peoples and republics struggled for lost freedom and an independence that was justified historically, politically and morally. Such is the view established in the West, it seems to me, as the only correct one. A different opinion voiced inside the country is regarded as the minimum legacy of conservatism. But such a simple reading of the situation does not fit in with the facts and the norms of the law. You don't like the laws? Then change them by democratic means, and then act in accordance with them. Otherwise what sort of establishment of the rule of law are we talking about?

This is by no means just the point of view of an inveterate dogmatist, an incorrigible conservative or a reactionary. I beg you to excuse me for relying once again on the authority of Aleksandr Yakovlev, but since no one can accuse him of being undemocratic or unprogressive, I will remind you: Yakovlev spoke out more than once about, for example, the unlawful actions undertaken by the leaders of the Baltic states and the forces calling for the separation of those states from the USSR by means of pressure and force contrary to the laws of the Soviet Union. These statements of his passed unnoticed or were deliberately suppressed.[30]

As well, however unpopular it may be, we must point out that all the acts connected with the dissolution of the USSR and the efforts to create the Union of Independent States were questionable from the point of view of legality. There is a popular saying that victors are not judged, and so today the people we regard that way are not judged. But how do we know forces will not emerge who will want to review everything that was done contrary to the law? It will not be the chauvinists, the imperialists, or the neo-Communists. No, those people are now quickly silenced ideologically and then politically. The question will be posed either by nationalist forces or by some new pretenders to power, with the aim of discrediting existing authorities. Ultimately, it is not important who raises the challenge first. What matters is how, according to what reasoning and what frontiers, the division of that enormous country formerly known as Russia was carried out. This question will for many long years produce politicians and movements, Russian or non-Russian, who will want to continue the argument.

People may, of course, exclaim that these are old thoughts, at the very least! How could one appeal to the laws of the USSR and the Constitution of the USSR if that state was undemocratic? Moreover, how would it be possible in the future to refer to these documents of a state that no longer existed? These are important points, and I too wish sincerely that the next generation would not try to settle accounts with history. But there are, unhappily, few examples in history bearing witness to a period of calm and quiet succeeding a slapdash solution of questions affecting frontiers or territory. As for referring to the laws of the Union, I would tell our indignant democrat to calm down. That is not my political position. But as a historian and political scientist I think it my duty to point out that we have no guarantee these questions won't arise. (Incidentally you can subject political and juridicial arguments to a similar kind of doubt while dispensing with such unquestionably democratic documents as what Professor Sakharov wrote in 1988 and 1989: his "Pre-Election Program," his draft "Decree About Power" and "The Constitution of the Union of Soviet Republics of Europe and Asia.")[31]

A final point. The paradoxes in our democratization process are very striking. Everybody placed their hopes in a referendum as the most democratic way of solving our problems, but when they announced a nationwide referendum on the question of whether the USSR should continue, the most important "democrats" and "democratic governments" voted either against it or against its results.

Historians, and even before the historians, the politicians and ordinary citizens, will understand and declare at the top of their voices that the collapse of the Union became irreversible after the leadership of the RSFSR (the Russian Federation) adopted their present position. Russia provoked the policy adopted by Ukraine, and Ukraine's position completely deprived Gorbachev of any chance of reanimating the Novo-Ogarevo process. This might be left to history, if not for two points. First, they say that an overwhelming majority of the population of Ukraine voted in favor of independent statehood on December 1, 1991. Yes, but roughly the same number of people voted in favor of a Ukraine within the USSR only six months previously (March 1991). Now, much water flowed under the bridge in that short period and the reversal in the new referendum was the result. And if more water flows? Another referendum? Or, God save us, will somebody come along who will prefer to resolve the problem by other means?

My second point is that the examples of the Chechen republic, Tatarstan, and other national regions in the Russian Federation show that the logic of Russia's policy towards the USSR may be applied in turn by Russian republics towards Russia. That means chaos, not only within the frontiers of Russia. Of course, for every right-thinking person, this is the worst solution. Perhaps for once good sense will prevail over reckless behavior.

Fears and doubts over ethnic relations began in December 1986 with the first political crisis over the nationality question — the events in Alma-Ata. Today, when the Soviet Union has been dissolved, it seems that either the USSR was incapable of being reformed and was doomed to collapse, or the policy of reform did not adequately reflect reality or came too late. For critics of the Soviet system the choice is obvious, because the USSR was the last empire and the last colonial power and so the Union was doomed. It seems to me that there was a path for renewal that did not involve the collapse and ruin of the USSR. It need not have remained hypothetical; it could have become real if Perestroika had included a wider variety of connections and a rejection of the one-dimensional type of relations between the republics.

However, that kind of idea was received officially with great hostility. I recall how difficult it was to introduce this thesis into articles even in 1989 and 1990, although I formulated the problem at an extremely theoretical and political level. There was a great deal of inertia here. Even references to Lenin did little to help, though by the end of his life he had come to believe a monolithic Union and a single type of development was an unacceptable model. In the end the leaders arrived at an understanding of the need for not only federative but also confederative, associational links between the republics and states, but it was already too late for it to happen within the framework of the USSR. The post-coup process moved things in the direction that Mikhail Heller forecast when he wrote, "A sovereign Russia would mean the emergence of a sovereign Ukraine and then the collapse of the last empire of the twentieth century."[32] So far this has proved to be true.

Naturally, the question arises, how did Gorbachev regard all this?

In the first place I am convinced that for a long time the country's leaders did not have a policy for Union reform. All they would say was that we had to free ourselves of the Stalinist legacy, be more democratic, and so forth, but there was no strategic plan for a step-by-step advance towards a given target. On the other hand, the nationalist and separatist forces knew what they wanted and how to get results. Gorbachev and his supporters in the Novo-Ogarevo process were able, it seemed, to correct the situation in the spring and summer of 1991, but the coup muddled up the cards. The investigation and the trial of the Committee for the Emergency ought to reveal what was behind the torpedoing of the Union treaty at that time, because the explanations to be heard today are far from convincing me. At any rate, after the coup, the nationalist movements practically everywhere joined up with the people in power and with the first leaders of the republic-states.

In the second place, it seems to me—and I make this judgment on the basis of an analysis of facts as well as personal observations—that, just as they had exaggerated ideas of the people's socialist convictions and sympathies, the political leadership of the USSR also overestimated what they called the "indestructible friendship of the peoples" and the strength and permanence of the links between the republics. It was difficult not to be surprised, for example, at the way Gorbachev tried during his 1990 visit to persuade Lithuania to drop the idea of leaving the USSR. He was very frank and argued his case well, and he was well received personally, but it was a dialogue between a politician and a public that seemed to talk different languages. As we say in such situations, the train had already left.

Similarly, until very recently Mikhail Sergeyevich would often argue that Russia and Ukraine should not separate, that Russians and Ukrainians should remain united, and he would often talk about the way the two nationalities were intermixed in his own family. Of course he had arguments that were not simply about what blood flowed in his veins or about his grandparents. He had plenty of persuasive facts from the realm of history, economics and culture about the ancient links between the peoples and the fact that now everything was interconnected. But his repeated reference to his own family perplexed people. People simply ridiculed him openly for it. I remember the surprise in some of our writers' eyes when Gorbachev began to talk about it at a meeting devoted to Dostoevsky's one-hundred-and-seventieth birthday in November 1991. A few days later there was to be a referendum in Ukraine, and the outcome of the voting in favor of independence for the Ukraine was a foregone conclusion. Once against the President started to talk about the Russian and Ukrainian ancestors in his family. He had a quite genuine conviction that the people around him could not fail to be inspired with the same feelings and the same understanding. After the meeting three people who had been present at the conversation asked me in a tone of wonderment and alarm, "Does the President really not see what the situation is, does he really rely on such romantic ideas and arguments?"

For me it really was a riddle. No, Gorbachev did not underestimate the danger of nationalist and separatist tendencies. He spoke about it more than once in public, and the formulations and evaluations made at various "limited" conferences were quite precise. During a meeting with a group of assistants in March 1991, after the referendum that gave impressive support to the President's policy of preserving the Union, he said that we must rely on the support of the people but not to draw any far-reaching conclusions from the results of the referendum—people were waiting for the practical evidence. But once again the weight of practical deeds proved insufficient for him to carry out his policy.

Nowadays, you can read incredibly divergent accounts of what is called Gorbachev's "political behavior." They often contain hints and sometimes outright accusations aimed at him. The most widely accepted of these would seem to be that he was too flexible and ready to compromise with people with whom to compromise is almost immoral, particularly the CPSU and its leaders. Discussing the problems of Gorbachev's policy on nationalism as a principal reason for his fall from power, Anatoli Sobchak, mayor of St. Petersburg and one of the most prominent democratic leaders, wrote in 1991: "Having become a hostage to reaction, [Gorbachev] ceased to be the democrat and the reformer he had been. So the General Secretary triumphed over the President.

"Tbilisi, Baku and the Baltic states. Those three milestones determined the personal drama of Mikhail Gorbachev as well as the fate of Perestroika which began so brilliantly in the mid-1980s."[33]

I have to agree that the three milestones he refers to were of very great importance, but it seems a subjective decision to leave out Nagorny Karabakh, Samarkand, events in Moldova and others. Mikhail Sergeyevich himself described very well such attempts to see and to defend only "one's own truth." But more important, I will never agree that Gorbachev at some stage of Perestroika ceased to be a democrat and a reformer. It simply did not happen. And if one democrat or another understood some situation differently than did the democrat Gorbachev, that is no reason for one side to scorn the other as conservative or reactionary.

Of course Gorbachev was not living and acting in a vacuum. He was obliged to take account of the realities in the country and the distribution of political forces. But while he entered into compromises, in the end Gorbachev never followed anyone's lead. It even seemed to me at times that he was organically incapable of taking over someone else's ideas as his own. No sooner had some new idea been voiced or published by someone else than it had to be worked over until it was unrecognizable so as to become Gorbachev's. He was not capable of plagiarism in politics. It was not just a matter of pride, as people sometimes imagine, though there was something of that. The most important thing was that as a strong-willed, thoughtful and independent person he had to have everything pass through him. Irrespective of the person involved, that kind of process always involves at least two hidden dangers—lost time, and the possibility of the original version being spoiled—just as it provides an opportunity to weigh everything carefully and to improve on an idea.

As for the notorious question of whether General Secretary Gorbachev gained the upper hand over President Gorbachev, let me tell you my opinion. After the first Congress of People's Deputies (June 1990), the introduction of the post of president (March 1990) and the changes that took place in the leadership at the 28th Congress of the Party (July 1990), nobody was in a position to dictate to Gorbachev. He could not fail to reckon with the real political forces, among which the CPSU was by no means the least, but there had been for some time nobody in the Politburo with whom Mikhail Sergeyevich had to reckon. He was free to act as his reason and conscience prompted him. Within the framework he thought correct, that is, a policy of the center-left, Gorbachev pursued his policy of reforming society, and it was impossible to divert him from it by constitutional or legal means. That's why the attempt to win him over in August 1991 was unconstitutional. That was why, at the end of 1991, he was led to resign, because the dissolution of the Union state of which he was president was carried out contrary to the procedures laid down in the Constitution.

To return to Solzhenitsyn's warning, only time will tell whether we shall succeed in creating on the territory of the former Soviet Union a set of states whose structure will take the peoples' traditions into account. This is not the only condition for a democratic and stable state system, but it is an indispensable one.

*"The New Thinking . . . a view of the world through the eyes of humanity."*

These are the words of Eduard Shevardnadze, who from practically the beginning of the Gorbachev era (July 1985) until the last days of the Soviet Union was in charge of the country's foreign policy. There was only one short interruption, from the end of 1990 to the autumn of 1991, caused by his resignation. He wrote a book titled *My Choice: In Defense of Democracy and Freedom*, which is well known in Russia and throughout the world. Being a person who has never been concerned professionally with international affairs, I want to draw the reader's attention to Shevardnadze's insights about the "new thinking" and what Gorbachev and his team achieved internationally.

The words I began this section with come from the following context in *My Choice*:

The 'new thinking' is a view of the world through the eyes of humanity and its interests. 'Man is the measure of all things.' From this point of view the new thinking is far from new. It is new only in the sense that an orientation towards the well-being of the human being is becoming today a greater political imperative.

Is that just idealism? Perhaps it is. But if we reject it we will have to acknowledge that the only correct policy is one that excludes individuals, their safety and their well-being from its main guidelines. It would be a policy that sacrificed the individual to false and selfishly interpreted national interests.

The architects of policy generally operate in categories that leave no room for the human being. There is 'the people,' 'the country' and 'national security' and that is the sum of the main categories, which overlook, however, the most important little matter—human life. As though it were self-evident that the collective approach will guarantee everyone's prosperity. But even in the most prosperous, well-planned and beautifully-built city, many of its citizens live in poor conditions. A policy should fit the human being.[34]

This was the philosophy behind the reorganization of Soviet foreign policy, developing mutual relations and changing the character of its links and the atmosphere prevailing over its contacts with the nations which are most important in deciding the political climate of our planet. The changes that have taken place in the world, in no small degree because of Perestroika, the new thinking and the policy of Gorbachev, are really tremendous.

Without going into the fairly well-known facts concerning world events in recent years, I will highlight the most important perceptions of Gorbachev's foreign policy leadership. Speaking of his "gift for analyzing and publicizing" and his "outstanding ability," Abdurakhman Avtorkhanov wrote in 1988:

> His ability as a speaker alone, which he borrowed from bourgeois legal debating, has enabled Gorbachev to perform political and psychological miracles. . . . Who could have guessed that such a convinced anti-Communist as President Reagan would, after meeting Gorbachev, drop his famous description of the USSR as 'the Evil Empire'? And what about the ordinary citizens? According to an opinion poll in Europe which asked which of the world's political leaders deserved the greatest confidence politically,

Gorbachev came out on top . . . [one] American woman declared firmly and categorically that 'the emergence of Mikhail Gorbachev is the second coming of Jesus Christ!'[35]

No reports or descriptions, even on film or television, give a real impression of how Gorbachev was greeted by people in various countries. I had the good fortune to observe such encounters in the USA, Canada, Norway, and Sweden. This was in 1990 and 1991, when the problems of Perestroika and Gorbachev's situation were providing ground for ever more insistent questions about the possible collapse of his policy and his regime, yet I was still able to experience the atmosphere attributed by Raisa Gorbachev to a trip to Italy in 1989:

> Italy, the country of Dante and Petrarch. Monuments everywhere to a great culture. The Cathedral Square in Milan with the amazingly beautiful decorated marble facade of the cathedral itself. And the equally amazing outpouring of emotion by the many, many thousands of people gathered there as the people of Milan welcomed Mikhail Sergeyevich and the delegation. 'Gorby! Gorby! Gorby!' they were shouting in the square. Eduard Amvrosyevich Shevardnadze and I were walking side by side. We had been left behind by Mikhail Sergeyevich and had to make our way through the dense crowd of people. I looked at him and saw that there were tears in his eyes, as there were in mine. He said to me then, 'For the sake of this, too, it was worthwhile to begin Perestroika.'[36]

For myself, I will always remember the faces in the ovation that greeted Gorbachev at his Nobel lecture on June 5, 1991, after an unusual incident. As he was reading his lecture in that ancient chamber in the capital of Norway, Gorbachev's voice was suddenly interrupted by very loud shouts. A woman stood up from the seats immediately in front of us and tried to force her way through to the President. She got past both the Norwegian and the Soviet security men, who were taken by surprise. People were shocked. What was she up to? Finally the security men did what was required.

When we exchanged opinions and impressions about the incident in the Soviet delegation and with the Norwegians, many of us agreed that in those few seconds we had recalled the recent assassination of Rajiv Gandhi. It was later explained to us that in fact there had been a couple, a woman and a man belonging to one of the tendencies in the Afghan opposition. (The man had shouted something from the back of the hall when he was removed.)

That was the situation: the silence of the grave interrupted by shouts. Some person trying to cover the ground to Gorbachev as fast as possible. A shocked pause. The Nobel prize winner himself interrupts his lecture and looks in surprise at what is going on. The security men seize the woman and take her quickly out of the hall. How long did it all last? A minute? A minute and a half? Then the calm voice of Gorbachev saying, "I will continue," followed immediately by a stormy ovation from the whole audience. Then again Gorbachev's voice cutting the applause short. Still more applause at the end.

The people attending the Nobel lecture were applauding a politician who had already achieved a great deal and who had set out his political beliefs, and they applauded the man for his courage and self-possession.

In the former Soviet Union today, quarrels frequently break out over foreign policy in the Perestroika period. To understand why, think of the alarm the world has felt since the collapse of the USSR about the problem of control over nuclear weapons. For Soviet people, such anxieties began long ago, as the new foreign policy required a reinterpretation of the impressions people had acquired over the years about the geopolitical distribution of forces, Eastern Europe's relations with the Soviet Union and so on. People do not find it easy to adopt new ways of thinking, if they are people and not just soulless machines capable of accepting the word of whomever may have the upper hand at the time.

Shevardnadze, too, says, "You come to the new thinking having experienced in your heart and mind the experience and lessons of the past." A few pages later, he speaks frankly of being on a flight from Geneva to Moscow with aides after the signing of agreements about Afghanistan, including the withdrawal of Soviet troops.

The stewardess brought us some wine and one of my assistants poured it into glasses, saying, 'To today's success!' But I could not take a sip. I felt very depressed. I could see in my mind the faces of my friends in Kabul. Now there was no one they could count on apart from themselves. Could they hold out after our troops had departed? How could we help them to achieve national reconciliation, put an end to the bloodshed and restore peace in Afghanistan? Thoughts of the people who had put their trust in us and who were now left to face their bitter enemies alone gave me no peace. I know that we would not reduce our political effort to achieve a peaceful settlement in Afghanistan; nevertheless I could not rid myself of a feeling of personal guilt towards my friends.[37]

Many human lives were destroyed in other countries during those years as well. That, too, is international policy "on a human scale."

# 8

# Gorbachev's Algorithm

M any mistakenly take the view that the prince in ruling a country and every nobleman in the conduct of his affairs ought above all to take account of the interests of the parties; but at the same time the supreme wisdom decrees that one should, on the contrary, conform either to the common interest, thus bringing about what representatives of the most differing parties agree with, or to the interests of separate individuals. By that I do not mean to say, however, that party considerations ought to be completely ignored. People of low rank must have something to hold onto in order to raise themselves; but people of high rank, aware of their strength, are better off preserving their independence. And, to be more certain of success, it is usually better for someone who is beginning to move up to display such moderate support so as to be, of all the members of his party, the one most acceptable to the other. —Francis Bacon, *Novum Organum*.[1]

Fortunate is he who has arranged his life in such a way that it corresponds with the peculiarities of his character, his wishes and his way of life, and so derives pleasure from his very existence. World history is not an arena of happiness. Periods of happiness appear like empty sheets of paper because they are periods of harmony and the absence of conflict. Reflection within oneself is a freedom. —Hegel, *The Philosophy of History*.[2]

What am I? What have I done? I have collected and made use of everything I have seen, heard or observed. My works are the product of thousands of different individuals, ignoramuses and wise men, clever people and stupid ones, childhood, maturity and old age —all have contributed to me their thoughts, their abilities, their hopes and their way of life. I have often harvested what others sowed; my work is the labor of a collective being that is called Goethe. —J. W. Goethe, *Maxims and Thoughts*.[3]

Politics is a game. Of all the children's games it is the most childish; of all the 'golden coverlets of day' it is the most transparent. If life is a shadow then politics is the shadow of a shadow; if life is a dream then politics is a dream within a dream. What can we ask of it? What will keep the child happy? —D. S. Merezhkovsky, "Two Secrets of Russian Poetry."[4]

The exhausting race with time and the stubborn resistance put up by the conservatives force him to speed up the movement ahead. This gives rise to fresh contradictions when the old ones do not merge into concrete steps forward along the path of reform. Consensus and dissatisfaction, support and criticism are thus always in a state of instability, while the things he has started need a long time to become effective and rely on wide and continual support. It is around this dilemma that the fate of Perestroika may be decided, and meanwhile Mikhail Gorbachev will have, as somebody shrewdly pointed out, to go on playing at the same time the role of Luther and that of Pope of Rome. Not to leave him in isolation in such a different enterprise may be of decisive importance for everybody. —Antonio Rubbi, *Meetings with Gorbachev*.[5]

The most important thing is not to give in now at this most critical point, not to stop and not to seek salvation behind us — that would be the greatest and fatal mistake. It would be suicide if on this occasion, as in the 1950s and 1960s, we faltered and stopped halfway. Then we would start slipping backwards.

It is true, everything has to mature. But for us now time is running out. We must not get into a panic or lose our heads. We must keep a cool head, be self-controlled and brave. But we must also preserve the quality of our thinking and the acuity with which we perceive contradictory processes. And, of course, our faith in the cause we have set in motion. —M. S. Gorbachev, *The August Coup*.[6]

In studying the imperatives of the Perestroika years, there is every reason to consider the period under the sign of the initiator and leader of those six and a half years of reforms. Gorbachev was not only the man who personified the changes, nor just the statesman and politician who headed the reforms. No, Mikhail Sergeyevich determined the content, the direction and the speed of Perestroika.

In this connection I would like to refer to my book on the history of the USSR, *When the Stars Fade*, because its description of these processes is quite different. At the time I underestimated the depth and scope of the influence of Gorbachev's personality on Perestroika. It seemed to me that the country would continue fundamentally to follow the path opened up by Gorbachev even after he departed. However, there is no country in which Perestroika continued long after it was started. Economic and social policy followed other guidelines both in Russia and in practically all the former union republics which are now independent states. Other social ideas determine the political atmosphere in our country. That is no longer Perestroika, but another, post-Perestroika life. And it is too soon yet to define it.

Before I continue, I must say that I have read reminiscences or even volumes of memoirs by prominent politicians of ours who have marched in step with each other and with Gorbachev and who have parted from each other and from their leader, having criticized him in the past and criticizing him even more today. I cannot rid myself of the feeling that they have brought their judgments up to date. This does not call everything in their memoirs into question, and I believe it is immoral to automatically gainsay someone's views that way. Nevertheless a great deal will remain a riddle until we have in our hands a history of Perestroika written by Gorbachev himself, and until the published documents and those still hidden in the archives have been analyzed by scrupulous historians.

One of our most distinguished theater critics, E. P. Simonov, told me once about a remarkable actor and producer, N. P. Akimov, a sharp-witted person who loved making up aphorisms. One of his sayings was that the most impossible thing to do in life was to write your memoirs at the beginning and then try to live your life in accordance with them. This serves as a fine warning to anyone who judges the main characters of history by the results of what they tried to do. The presumption of innocence, it seems to me, does not apply only to the law but to history too. And there it extends to such aspects as the purity and morality of intentions. They say, of course, that the road to Hell is paved with good intentions, but in history it is practically impossible to prove that a different path from the one chosen would have been less difficult and less dramatic. History, of course, does not pardon outright crimes, but that is not what's at issue.

To understand how Perestroika came specifically out of the special characteristics of Gorbachev as a leader, we need to examine at least four subjects. First, how the problems facing society compare with the leader's interpretation of them. Second, the distribution of the principal political forces in society and their interests. Third, how priorities are chosen in policy making and how decisions are taken aiming at achieving set targets. Finally, the adequacy of policy to meet the practical demands of society.

Of course, to answer these questions comprehensively would take more space than is appropriate here, and to answer them briefly would be to do them an injustice. I set myself a much more modest task: to try to provide an outline and an assessment of the key problems as I see them.

As I've said before, by the middle of the 1980s, Soviet society was in such a state that most people realized it could not go on that way. What's more, it was clear that not a single influential politician or grouping of any importance that was opposed in principle to a long-term policy of renewal, or what came to be known as Perestroika. The leaders of the country were persuaded of the need to reform socialism. And there were no recorded serious differences when it came to the point where people saw a need for economic reform.

By about 1987, though, it was obvious that two tendencies had formed within the ruling bodies, identified respectively with the names of Ligachev and Yakovlev. Gorbachev occupied centrist positions, supporting each side on different occasions, as a fairly visible struggle for influence over him went on at the middle level of the administration. Nevertheless, even then there were no conflicts likely to produce a real disaster, because, after all, the point was the need to get rid of the traces of Stalinism, to democratize public life, and so forth. But the actual extent of the reforms both in the economy and in political life were understood by many in different ways. Somewhere about the middle of 1988 the process of crystallizing the differences had reached such a level that it became impossible to bring together opposing views, even through the efforts of such a master of compromise as Gorbachev. It may be that the most effective factor in setting the two extremes apart was the switch of functions in the Politburo. Ligachev and Yakovlev, who had previously both been dealing with ideology, were transferred to handling, respectively, agriculture and international affairs. Ideology was handed over to V. A. Medvedev, a centrist by character and by conviction.

This period from mid-1987 to mid-1988 is regarded as crucial in the progress of Perestroika, and Yakovlev avoided making major decisions concerning economic and political reforms in June 1987 and then in June 1988.[7] By the end of 1989 and the summer of 1990, as indicated in the following assessments, many explosive problems had piled up in the storehouses of irreconcilable politicians.

Boris Yeltsin:

> Incidentally, however strange it may seem, the number of issues of principle that the so-called right-wingers and left-wingers disagree about is not great. Probably the most important is the question of ownership. To recognize private or individual, whatever you call it, ownership of property would bring about the collapse of the main bastion that supports the state monopoly over property and everything connected with it—the power of the state, the alienation of the individual from his own labor and so on. The second issue which is probably no less important is the question of land.... Then there is the devolution of authority, the economic independence of the republics and real sovereignty. The removal of all restrictions on the economic, financial and managerial independence of enterprises

and labor collectives. The restoration of the country's financial situation is tied up with the measures I have mentioned, but special financial measures are still necessary to avoid the complete collapse of the ruble.[8]

Y. K. Ligachev:

> During the preparations for the 28th Congress of the Party, when the theses of the main report were being discussed. . . . Yakovlev and Medvedev continued to put forward conservatism as the main danger [to Perestroika]. I sent Gorbachev my written opinion, in which I pointed out that there were at least three main dangers: conservatism, national separatism and the forces that were pushing the country towards a bourgeois system. I tell you frankly, as I understand it, in my opinion conservatism is not the main danger for Perestroika. But over this question I accepted a political compromise, because for me the most important thing was to point to the danger of nationalism.
>
> Unfortunately the danger of a revival of nationalist forces featured in the report only as a 'serious complication' in carrying out the tasks of Perestroika. In other words, even in mid-1990, when the process of destroying the USSR had started, people still minimized the main danger—national separatism.[9]

In a period of violent change, events that at other times would take decades get compressed into a single year, and there was less than two years between these two statements. However, it must be said that the key problems of Perestroika were confronted. In the end the solution of the disputes about ownership, as the future President of Russia had predicted, led to the country's refusal to advance further along the lines of our traditional idea of socialism. Today we have already gone further in transforming property relations, at least in our planning. The tensions which Ligachev stressed ended in the collapse of any hope of preserving the Union and in the unpredicted forms of "divorce" between the former Soviet republics. People often say, in reference to family quarrels, that "it was love without joy, so the separation will be without sorrow." But things are not quite so simple in relations between whole peoples, and the ancient links between them cannot be reduced to just two emotions, love and sorrow.

The realization of the hopes and threats addressed by

Yeltsin and Ligachev turned out to lie beyond the limits of Perestroika. You could say that in 1991 Gorbachev himself came to recognize the need for private ownership, but in his case the idea was always qualified, always an obvious compromise with earlier, allegedly socialist principles, until the coup. Even in the article he wrote in Foros before the August events there is reference to a mixed economy, changeovers of economic ways of life and economic freedom. But there is also a warning against the dangers of headlong, thoughtless "capitalization." Only on the pages dealing with the "Lessons of the Coup" do we read of the need to offer complete freedom to private enterprise, the rapid creation of institutes for the study of market economics and the transfer of land to all who are willing to cultivate it, without any limitations. As for the collapse of the USSR, Gorbachev continually emphasized that he had no intention of presiding over a break-up. He remained an advocate of a renewed Union state—but fate would have it that the President would quit his post only after the announcement of the dissolution of the USSR.

Second: I am convinced that Gorbachev's assessments and perceptions of the Union's problems were adequate, but only so long as events were controlled by Gorbachev, and political movements and leaders already in a position to dictate terms to him did not gather strength. By character he was a man incapable not only of using dictatorial measures, but even of resorting to hard-line administrative means. The logic of social growth led to a situation in which he was unable to take the lead in further reforms, because he could not reject his essential values.

Ligachev, who describes himself as a realist, called his book *The Riddle of Gorbachev*. In one of his interviews Yakovlev commented bitterly, "I am a romantic and I consider Gorbachev to be a great and tragic figure." Both authors are politicians who worked alongside Gorbachev for several years, and I believe that between them they reveal what history will call the Gorbachev phenomenon.

I have often wondered how it was possible for this one man to be at the same time a realist capable of discerning the country's problems and an absolute idealist—how to assess the degree of inertia of society, the forces of resistance to change and the degree of responsibility of the leader, his real chances of success and his possibilities?

In politics, to control events often means controlling the people who stand behind them, or at least neutralizing those people. Mikhail Sergeyevich Gorbachev is a person endowed by nature with magnetic qualities. He is capable of carrying challengers along with him, amusing and disarming his interlocutor by his conviction and the art of persuasion. It was not only because Gorbachev could not or would not listen that people from his "team" left him. That certainly happened, but as far as I understand it, it happened mostly when something extremely important was lacking to sway the President's attentions—when there was a lack of character. In this connection I am no exception. I asked twice to be allowed to leave and return to work at my specialty. Both times I took my request back and stayed.

One of my most memorable encounters with Gorbachev was my first in informal circumstances, which is perhaps what makes it memorable. The First Congress of People's Deputies had begun; fierce debates were taking place. Everything was happening for the first time, everything was unusual. But Gorbachev had a promise to fulfill, and during an interval he went to call on Leonid Maximovich Leonov, a living treasure of Russian literature. He went to congratulate the writer on his ninetieth birthday, and he stayed not just for his scheduled 15 to 20 minutes but for more than an hour. It was an amazingly concentrated and interesting conversation, and there were toasts and jokes. But there was one special moment.

Leonov repeated Gorbachev's own words—that Perestroika, which he had originated, was due to change the country fundamentally and would exert an influence on its development for two or even three hundred years. Now, I know writers, artists, and politicians who have criticized Gorbachev and opposed him, some from the right and some from the left, and some among them reacted to this episode roughly like this: there's Gorbachev boasting again, lavishing compliments on his own Perestroika. But I, having had the opportunity to discuss this several times with Leonov, know that on this occasion this wise man rose above his politicized colleagues and the politicians and did not make his judgment according to his own tastes. Instead, it was as if he were being a prophet in his diagnosis. His talent and his experience of life as a creative writer enabled him to detect the far-reaching consequences of the transformations that were only beginning to take place. And he welcomed them.

You can argue as much as you please about what the leaders of Perestroika foresaw and what happened spontaneously because of deeper elemental processes. Either way, those leaders, including Gorbachev, clearly wanted to do good for the people and make them happy, and they decided that the only way to do it was through a radical restructuring of society. Each one understood this in his own way.

Perhaps all Russian reformers really do have tragic fates. Perhaps it is only tyrants and the talentless who die peacefully, only to be cursed when they have reached another world.

We must bear in mind the factual data we have on the mood prevailing in society during Perestroika. In the most general terms, I agree with those Soviet and Western researchers who say that dividing social groups and strata into those who were for and against Perestroika is difficult, but that all the same the great majority have been supporters of the restructuring of society.

Tatyana Zaslavskaya, in 1988, sketched out the different sectors: the originators of Perestroika, who came from the

December 1991, the end of Mikhail Gorbachev's reign. At the last meeting of the President with his aides and advisers, two days before his resignation, from left facing the camera: Vladimir Yegorov, Georgi Pryachtin, Vadim Medvedev, and Alexander Yakovlev.

radically inclined parts of the leadership, the intelligentsia and the politically active; the supporters of Perestroika, who could be found in every stratum, particularly "workers, peasants and small entrepreneurs"; the quasi-supporters, mostly amongst the bureaucrats; the neutral, mostly manual workers and peasants; conservatives, found again at every level but particularly among the better-off workers, small businesspeople and collective farmers; and the "outright reactionaries," whom she finds "concentrated in a limited number of groups to which special attention should be given in the process of directing Perestroika. That means, firstly, the corrupted part of the officials working in the party and Soviet *apparat*; secondly, highly placed employees in trade and retail business; thirdly, a section of the working class bribed by the previous groups; and, finally, people active in organized crime."[10]

Her conclusion is that Perestroika was not a revolution by one social group against another, but a contest of ideas in which the "real frontier does not run so much 'between the lines' as 'between the columns' of the matrix . . . with the increasing involvement in the struggle of groups that have still not made up their minds."[11]

The subsequent course of events and the following years demonstrated the correctness of this analysis. This type of social transformation was maintained at every stage of Perestroika. It was roughly speaking a confrontation of radicals and conservatives, not a revolutionary restructuring.

For a long time, though, the imperatives of Perestroika were determined only in the upper reaches of society. The people remained silent and have still not spoken out much even now, although, of course, they were not completely invisible, if you remember the worst of the strike movements in the summer of 1989 and the spring of 1991 and the support given by the masses to the democratic forces during the attempted coup. However, it must not be said that the coup leaders themselves received considerable mass support, and "the whole country" did not respond to Yeltsin's appeal for a general political strike.

I believe that Gorbachev saw the true extent to which the idea of Perestroika had penetrated the people. He realized that it was not the mass social forces that would lead the campaign but the avant garde groups and strata in society. His statements and his actions bear witness to that. It is essentially only in the last two years that his speeches have begun to include the theme that Perestroika is increasingly affecting the fundamental interests of millions of people, which is why the struggle is becoming more violent.

But, as the reader will recall, in such key questions as the attitude to be adopted to the socialist period of Russian history, to socialism in general, to the changes leading to the development of private enterprise, and so forth, public opinion was becoming ever more critical and tilted toward liberal values. It is simply that the masses reached the point of "coming out on the streets" and off the sidelines only when discontent with the material situation and the absence of tangible results from Perestroika on the shop shelves coincided with a critical reinterpretation of history and a reassessment of social values. The president's opponents and enemies responded to this fundamental shift in events much sooner than Gorbachev himself did.

One of the most striking indications of the president's declining authority was the way various groups in the creative and scientific intelligentsia distanced themselves from him. Many well-known cultural figures who had provided Gorbachev's most weighty and audible support in the first years of Perestroika began in the end of 1989 to move away for Gorbachev or even to join the opposition. This was an extremely confusing phenomenon, because the switch was expressed in various ways and there was no single position. Many groups of intellectuals would not even shake each other by the hand.

But this was a sort of sign or the herald of a coming storm. However much these people disagreed among themselves, as creative artists they understood sooner than others when politics got out of touch with the people and had a sharp eye for particular politicians' prospects. In any case people stopped queuing up to be received by Gorbachev. Of course, the president is the president and people did approach him and want to meet him, particularly those non-opportunists who had not been caught up in politics. They came to see him and invited him to their first nights, their shows and concerts. But the tendency was to move away, exacerbated by some people's dissatisfaction with the fact that Gorbachev would talk with their foes in the battle between the various groups in the professional societies—another aspect of the difficult problem of centrism in politics.

Another one of Gorbachev's troubles was the disadvantage of being in power rather than in opposition, especially against a background of a worsening economic situation and growing political instability. I agree with the Soviet philosopher V. Vyunitsky, who wrote in 1991:

> It has been said long ago and quite justly that Mikhail Gorbachev is a master of compromise who deliberately occupies a position at the center of balance. But there is need for greater precision here: it is not the balance of the political forces on the country but the balance of interests and tendencies of the groups who participate in the actual distribution of power. That means that his advisers are mainly various groupings in the party, state and economic *apparat*, whose main political skill is to agree interests.[12]

Right up to the end of Perestroika, the Soviet president's support—bubbling, unsettled, even shaky as it was—depended on the agreement of most of the republics and their leaders on the priority of preserving the Union. This was also the question on which, for the first and only time, Gorbachev decided to rely on the will of the people. The referendum in March 1991 about whether the USSR was to continue to exist or not demonstrated the correctness of that policy. Work on the new Union treaty strengthened his position.

At the same time it has to be remembered that it was not long before the referendum took place that the question of Gorbachev's resignation was first raised officially and openly by his most obvious rival, Boris Yeltsin. In a speech broadcast by the central television network on February 19, 1991, he declared:

> In the first two years after 1985, Gorbachev gave many of us a certain hope. . . . Having inspired people with hope, he began to operate by other laws. This became especially apparent recently when it became quite obvious that he wanted, while preserving the word 'Perestroika,' not to restructure anything fundamentally, but to preserve the system and the harsh centralized regime and not to allow the republics to be independent, especially Russia. It was in this that his policy started to be at odds with the people. It involved monetary manipulations, the planning of an unprecedented Pavlovian rise in prices, a sharp turn to the right, the use of the army against the civilian population, bloodshed in relations between the peoples, the collapse of the economy, a poor standard of living for the people, and so forth. There you have the result of six years of Perestroika—and that is what is most important.

I dissociate myself from the position and policy of the President; I am in favor of his immediate retirement and the transfer of power to a collective body—the Council of the Federation.[13]

I am sure this last proposal, not just demanding resignation but the transfer of power to an unconstitutional collective body, will be the subject of study by historians in the context of all the subsequent events, such as the attempt to remove the president from power by unconstitutional means in August, the changes to the Constitution and the dissolution of the USSR essentially by the signatures of people who presumably were due to compose Yeltsin's "Council of Federation." But to draw up such a policy while forgetting other facts would also be an invalid approach. After all, by the time the referendum was being held and Yeltsin was demanding Gorbachev's resignation, seven of the 15 republics had declared themselves against a Union center and the President's nationality policy. Obviously the most varied and contradictory processes were going on, including the most grave tactical and analytical mistakes made in developing inter-ethnic relations in the soon-to-be former USSR. Whatever was happening, it led to a point where consensus became impossible.

In the summer and autumn of this year, Gorbachev and the people closest to him in the official state bodies (i.e., "the Committee for the Emergency") and Boris Yeltsin and the forces backing him each made a choice. They also made their most powerful moves. So did the leaders of the republics, who fairly quickly dropped their neutral attitude in order to distance themselves from everybody—first from the Committee for the Emergency, then from Gorbachev and, finally, even from Yeltsin.

The future will show whether the people responsible for the fate of my people today will turn out to have been wiser and more successful than Gorbachev. And that alone will answer the question of whether they are historic personalities.

As for Gorbachev, he is definitely an historic figure, historic in the sense described by one of the outstanding Russian historians of the nineteenth and twentieth centuries, A. E. Presnyakov, who had another person in mind—the Russian Tsar Aleksandr I. If you look past the details in this description, you will see my understanding of Mikhail Sergeyevich Gorbachev, a man who had his own way of perceiving and understanding our period and acted accordingly:

> Aleksandr I was a truly historic figure, that is to say he was typical of his period, reflecting in himself the strength of accumulated traditions and the developing struggle with them, the struggle of various tendencies and interests, the general emotional tone of the period and its ideological trends. He reflected them . . . in the most difficult conditions, as the bearer of supreme authority in a period of the most strained external and internal struggle of such a typical 'transitional period' from the deeply shaken but still very strong old regime . . . to the maturing but still weak but insistently demanding new structure. . . . Aleksandr I was the 'born sovereign' of his country, as they said in olden days, educated to assume power and engage in political activity, totally absorbed by the thought of it from childhood, and at the same time a child of the eighteenth century and its ideological and emotional legacy, and he grew up and entered life for the arduous, responsible and tense role as the ruler at a stormy and difficult moment when there were revealed to the ruling circles the deep and burdensome contradictions of Russian reality. . . . A more receptive than creative temperament made him especially a man of his time. It is only against the background of the historical period that the individual psychology of such natures becomes at all comprehensible.[14]

Russian history is amazingly rich in such parallels.

My meditations bring me now to the problem of choice. Choice is not a simple exercise in arithmetic in which you add things up, make an estimate and take a decision. No, to choose is a matter of applying reason to all the possible alternatives, and if the first choice is to a large extent the result of intellectual effort, the second is unthinkable without psychologically difficult decisions. Of course, in real life all these "choices," intellectual and psychological, are mixed up among various people in a given situation.

It seems to me that the main choice, the one made in 1985,

was the easiest for Gorbachev and the other leaders of the country to make. It was due to be made. It was the successor to a way of living that had obviously outlived itself. This choice may have demanded some sacrifices, some virtues, but the later choices demanded very much more, as they broke up into such a number of possible variants that I doubt whether Gorbachev's critics and opponents, or even his supporters, always give much thought to their complexity.

My people are living today through a very strange period. Only yesterday a great deal seemed clear. We had enough of stagnation, so we chose Perestroika. We were disappointed with Perestroika, so we looked around for alternatives. And we found them—some of us chose to reject the policy of reform and even called openly for everything to be turned back; some thought it necessary to change our values in the process of restructuring society and the radicalization of the reforms; some sought and are still seeking some kind of palliatives or "unusual" solutions.

More and more I have the impression that while Gorbachev rejected categorically any return to the past, he did not make up his mind about the possible ways forward until the very end of his rule. Perhaps he rejected one way on grounds of reason. Another he found unacceptable psychologically. And to a third way he was unable to formulate his attitude because, however attractive it was, it did not fit in very well with our traditions. A fourth and a fifth variant were not very clearly sketched out and to back them in the great game of politics was simply naive. The leader lost his head. He became confused when the creative potential of Perestroika, in the light of previous experience, had exhausted itself.

He was capable of freeing himself from the cage of his own convictions, but that would take time. Neither history, nor his political opponents nor, most tragically, the people were ready to give him that time. Desperate efforts were made after the August coup to devise new policies in his name. But it was already too late. I believe the calmness with which the country reacted to the president's resignation was the hardest blow for him, though he was not immediately aware of it. In our last two conversations—one in person, another by telephone—I could sense his carefully concealed amazement at that circumstance, in my opinion, concealed even from himself. Perhaps from himself to the greatest extent.

Hegel made a brief and accurate diagnosis when he said, "Public opinion includes everything false and true, but to discover in it what is true is the work of a great man. The person who can say what his period of history wants, tells it and carries it out is a great man of his time. He carries out what amounts to the internal essence of the time and realizes its demands; he who is not able to scorn public opinion as it reaches his ears here and there will never perform anything great."[15] I don't know whether it happened for the first or the fifth time, but I dare to assert that in the most critical situations in 1991 Gorbachev did not display those qualities, that is he was not able to ignore what he had to listen to from here and there, from the left and from the right. His time of greatness became a time of tragedy and he was no longer able to halt that transition.

There was a period of greatness, though, and it triumphed for some five, almost six years. How those years will survive in the national memory and history will be not for our children but for our grandchildren and great-grandchildren to know. They will be able to study Perestroika soberly and calmly. They will have access to material now not available for study.

Vyunitsky, pondering Gorbachev's and Yeltsin's characters in early 1991, stated something true and perceptive:

> In the end the President and General Secretary of the CPSU, as the social and political basis of Perestroika shrank, became ever more dependent on a majority in the administration. This creates two problems for him. In the first place, since the distribution of trends in the administration differs from the way they are spread in society there is a danger of politics being divorced from reality. Such a situation makes great demands upon the political technologists and requires the continual adjustment of priorities

and political programs by real life. In the second place, increasing importance in such conditions is acquired by the organization of the institutions of power and the technology of their use. They become essential to the pattern of the President's actions.[16]

Any person, even one with little experience of politics, who sets this analysis alongside the events that followed will say they agree almost totally. Gorbachev did not succeed in extracting himself from dependence on the power structure right up to August 1991. He did it only after the coup, and then, having freed himself from dependence on the people around him, he deprived himself also of the support of the power structure at the very center. No other structure or machinery of power existed, as has been pointed out, and there was really no social basis for presidential rule. Resignation and a fall from power were predestined. There was only one question—when it would happen. It turned out that it took four months to complete the process.

Centrist policy, as I have said, is always accompanied by great difficulties. The president of the USSR understood that very well and sought new and unusual solutions. In principle he was accessible to new people and young researchers with original ideas, especially from the end of 1990. Some of these contacts took place through me, when Mikhail Sergeyevich asked me to support one of the researchers or to arrange cooperation with another. He had a feeling of approaching disaster. He was looking for a way out. But he was expecting a blow from the left, and the blow came from the right, from the people directly responsible for leading the country, the people closest to him. The coup upset all the cards in Gorbachev's political game.

"From whom do we get our support?" one of his assistants asked at a conference in November 1991. He formulated the answer himself—we have no basis in society. Seek, think—where is the solution? There was, however, no way out. In the language of chess, Gorbachev had run out of time after the August events. The moves were dictated by Yeltsin and other republican leaders who became heads of state. The "team" that was revived after the coup tried to save the game but the game had been changed—they were led off to do battle in a boxing ring or on a hockey field, and they did not know the rules.

Gorbachev chose his words well when he made his last speech on television. He said he "had ceased his activity in the post of President of the USSR." To talk of retiring would have made no sense: he could ask to be allowed to retire only at a Congress of People's Deputies of the USSR, and there was no USSR to have a congress about. The President did not take a decision, as he put it. He accepted the conditions dictated to him.

There arises, of course, the question of this new "team" that took the reigns in the selection of political priorities. There has been some analysis of this by political scientists, and much idle guessing, but a reply to this question—like those about the composition of the team, its quality, and how it worked—is impossible without the opinion of Gorbachev himself. So far he has said nothing, and I do not find it possible to indulge in fantasies. I will just say this:

For decades there existed in Soviet political practice a body whose approval was required for every decision that was taken. It was known as the Politburo of the Central Committee of the CPSU. It continued to exist right up until the dissolution of the party and was always headed by the General Secretary. But after the election of the President of the USSR and the repeal of Article Six of the Constitution of the USSR, the Politburo was deprived of its powers. Even more, the Politburo was no longer meeting regularly and it often did not even discuss the most important problems affecting the life of the country. This was quite natural in the period of democratization and the establishment of the rule of law.

The president then created, one after the other from 1989 on, such bodies as the Presidential Council, the Security Council, the Council of the Federation and finally the State Council. With all possible qualifications and exceptions not one of these bodies, apart from the State Council, had any power over the president.

Theoretically the General Secretary always could act independently of the Politburo, but only Stalin had actually done this. The removal of Khrushchev in 1964 was convincing evidence that such times had passed. To protect himself against such actions, Gorbachev rid himself of direct dependence upon a small circle of people. He secured himself against a possible "palace revolution"—but he brought an excessive load and responsibility on himself. Because he was by nature a democrat, he could not accept sole responsibility for making crucial decisions, which explained his continual striving to back up his policies by means of resolutions of the Supreme Soviet and the Congress of People's Deputies. Democratic though they were, these devices led to lost time and emasculated decisions. So his political choice turned out not to have adequate political guarantees.

Pondering questions of this kind while on holiday, he wrote:

> I am firmly convinced that problems can be resolved only by constitutional means. There is a weakness in this, but there is also strength. The strength is that society and humanity, having obtained freedom, have also obtained the possibility of realizing their democratic rights and this they value. The weakness derives from the fact that, when those rights are abused, it is very difficult to resort to the use of force even if it is lawful and justified. In this consists the specific nature of the process of Perestroika as a whole. It is not a matter of the President's powers but of the moral and political aim.[17]

Humanity, with all its strengths and weaknesses, was set above the president. If only there had been a similar subordination with relation to the Constitution it would have been possible to talk of assessing some of the instruments of power, even very high ones and especially that part of the team that consisted of advisers, assistants, and researchers. Mikhail Sergeyevich found it difficult to react to requests and demands that we should get together in "our own circle" to discuss problem as they arose. There were a few such meetings, but apart from two or three cases it all ended up as good intentions. In the president's *apparat* we spoke about this more than once and quite openly, but it seemed then as today that Gorbachev found it difficult to listen to other opinions in such groups. Perhaps our level and abilities did not suit him, which I think is possible, but what prevented him in that case from changing that part of the team? After all, there was no need for anybody's agreement to appoint fresh assistants or to dismiss old ones.

I don't know why such an unquestionably intelligent, experienced, and sensitive politician should adopt such a style in his work. In my view there simply is not a reasonable answer to that question. As I see it, it all lies in the realm of psychology, but no psychologist could understand it who had not experienced commensurable power and faced analogous problems. When will such a psychologist emerge? Ever? Without that, no attempt to understand this or that political choice in the course of Perestroika will be sufficient.

Three more questions. I have touched on each of them in one way or another already, but I think something remains to be said about them all.

The first concerns the actual phenomenon of the politician—reformer or revolutionary. I continue to assert that Gorbachev is a reformer. Only under the pressure of circumstances that did not depend on him, following the August events, did he agree that the transition taking place in life was not only being planned but was being put into practice through a revolutionary break with everything the country stood for before Perestroika. That was also a break with Perestroika. At that point the transformations moved to a qualitatively different level from what was declared to be the policy of Perestroika. What people in Russia and in the West like to call a "revolution from above" started in the autumn of 1991, but there was no room for Gorbachev in that process.

Both Soviet and foreign historians and political scientists (Litvak, Sirotkin, Heller, Laqueur, Tucker) compare Gorbachev's reforms with those of Aleksandr II, that other historic figure. The most important thing the Russian emperor did was to abolish serfdom in 1861. He explained his motives clearly in a speech made on the March 30, 1856, addressed to the nobility:

> There are rumors circulating that I intend to grant freedom to the peasants. That is not right and you can tell that to everybody to the right and the left; but hostile feelings exist, unfortunately, between the peasants and the landowners, and there have already been cases of refusal to obey the landowners. I am convinced that sooner or later we shall have to deal with this matter. I believe that you [the gentry] also share my opinion. Consequently it is much better that it should take place from above than from below.[18]

If you think about these statements you can understand that they are the words of a man with startling ideas for his time, but nonetheless a reformer. The landscape of Gorbachev's political actions is typologically similar. When the process moved downwards it became alien to the president, and he became alien to the process. I cannot imagine, even if I multiply by ten the flexibility and elasticity of Gorbachev's political thinking, that he would have done what Yeltsin is doing in Russia or what Kravchuk is doing in Ukraine. It would have gone against his very nature.

Gorbachev was capable of carrying out a revolution in his own head and in the minds of millions of his fellow citizens, but he was not capable of performing revolutionary acts. In revolutions, however, anyone may try to dress them up; there is no standing on ceremony with the people on the other side of the barricades. Mikhail Sergeyevich could act decisively, even unceremoniously, towards individual politicians. But he could not behave in the same way to parties, movements, social groups and strata.

In addition, neither "General Secretary Gorbachev" nor "President Gorbachev" were capable of heading a dictatorial regime. It is true that he asked for additional powers and was given them. It is also true that, as head of state, he could not fail to think about taking emergency measures, including the use of force, to defend the Constitution and the rule of law. I don't know how cynical you have to be to refuse the president the right to be faithful to his oath of office. That is why I consider that, in seeking the "hand of Gorbachev" behind the activities of the Committee for the Emergency, you cannot separate the problems of, on the one side, introducing a state of emergency and, on the other, the creation for that purpose of an anti-constitutional body. That is exactly how the question was posed, for example, by Oleg Shenin, former secretary of the Central Committee of the CPSU, in his statement to the Prosecutor of Russia when being questioned about the attempted coup d'état.[19]

Gorbachev could have introduced a state of emergency in accordance with the Constitution and there was a legal procedure for doing so. But he saw no reason for taking such a step. Otherwise there would have been no sense in the whole Novo-Ogarevo process, in which he had invested such sincere effort. He was really not going to commit suicide. I say quite openly that I was reduced to a state of confusion by Shevardnadze's statement at the time of the coup: "I am not totally convinced of his role and his fate," meaning Gorbachev's role in the attempted coup.[20] After all, that man knew the President very well. He was possibly one of his closest colleagues.

Yes, everybody knows the reasons for former Minister Shevardnadze's resignation and his repeated warnings about the threat of a dictatorship. But his motivation for doubting Gorbachev's role in the state of emergency on August 19 became clear to me after Shevardnadze made such amazingly mild comments about the regime established in Georgia by President Gamsakhurdia. It was such a regime that the country and the whole world trembled at its errant totalitarian nature, with sympathy for the people of Georgia.

I only mention this to reiterate my feelings about Mikhail Sergeyevich's inability to act as a dictator. However much a supporter of democracy a man may be it has to be admitted that to carry out profound reforms you need a strong will and a steadfast character. Sometimes even cruelty. In practice Mikhail Gorbachev either did not possess these qualities or deliberately suppressed them in himself so as to preserve the purity of the democratic process. But his democratic opponents resorted to such measures as soon as they had the opportunity. Practice demonstrated, at least in one country and at a specific time, that it is possible to carry out reforms without a dictatorship, but not without firmness or even toughness.

I want to sum up my reflections about the history of Russia and Perestroika by referring to one of our best-known philosophers, A. P. Butenko. In a recently published article, he wrote that we are not moving from socialism, which we have never really had in Russia, to civilized capitalism, but towards "savage capitalism . . . with all power in the hands of speculative capital and its unproductive bourgeoisie." In this light, he says, we can see the coup as an attempt by the bureaucrats to restore "barrack pseudo-socialism," but as we know it was defeated by a popular rising which propelled the "democrats" of the republics, led by Yeltsin, to a dominant position. This shift was marred, Butenko notes, by the fact that different republics were moving to very different paths, according to their own traditions and means—some much less prosperous and democratic than others.

For this reason, Butenko says:

> the return of Gorbachev from Foros and the restoration of his presidential authority in a national-democratic form was in fact an attempt to base the nationwide authority of yesterday on a mixed foundation of political systems in different republics that were moving further apart all the time. But the further things went the more the union regime itself became an obstacle to the process of further demarcation which had already gathered up some strength.
>
> The question arose of removing this obstacle, of relieving Gorbachev of his presidential power and of the closing down of institutions and organizations connected with it. . . . This role was played by the December anti-presidential 'three-way agreement' that was thought up and put into practice in Byelorussia. For the sake of getting rid of Gorbachev it abolished the USSR.

Finally, Butenko asks, "What about the future? Will the situation be saved by moves based on the old principle of 'the end justifies the means'—a community of republics and peoples described as a Commonwealth of Independent States? Hardly! . . . Is it not true that a worthy end can be achieved only by worthy means?"[21]

I do not wish to enter into a discussion of terminology, assessments of social and political forces, or opinions about the attitudes of republics and their leaders. Butenko is right about a lot of things. But it is important to stress that he is correct when he says that the Union was broken up in order to remove a deeply disappointing president. Not a single politician who signed the treaty creating the CIS will ever agree with that opinion, because to agree would be to pass sentence upon themselves. With one or two exceptions, these leaders did not want to see the Union break up. But nobody had the strength to oppose the process that was under way, while some people's anti-Gorbachev feelings overwhelmed the others, including their attitude to the state. This is the simple truth—simple for the politicians, but what was it like for the people?

In twentieth-century Russia there have been three leaders who were lawyers—Kerensky, Lenin and Gorbachev. Paradoxically, these were also the three men who placed the prospect of revolutionary reforms above the law. Historians can produce many examples of such moves by Kerensky and Lenin, but Gorbachev also appealed more than once for action in support of Perestroika contrary to the law, when the laws did not fit in with the interests of transforming the country. Moreover, while he threatened to use his powers to defend the Constitution, he certainly did not always do what was necessary for this defense.

It is not a question of whether the Constitution was a good one, or whether the laws were good or bad. The truth was that they either had to be observed or changed in good time.

There is something ominous in the unconstitutional way

Gorbachev was removed. Ominous and logical. I know how it happened, the actual procedure, from eye-witnesses who saw almost everything. I shall say only one thing here—it is difficult to imagine a more humiliating act at such a political level. If I had not myself been a witness of similar things I would not believe it.

In fact, as I wrote these lines I came to a halt and caught myself (not for the first time!) thinking that only a year ago, and certainly two, three, or five years ago, I could never have believed that what has taken place in my country could happen. Who could have imagined it? I am sure no one could. And that is quite normal, in the process of moving out of a dead-end into the unknown.

I will sum up by quoting one of the most brilliant politicians of our era, N. A. Nazarbayev, the President of Kazakhstan. In a book he finished writing in the spring of 1991, he wrote: "The confusion arose when people came face-to-face with the economic and state structure. Nobody knew for sure where to begin, what ought to be torn down and thrown away as being useless and what ought to be preserved and rebuilt."

He goes on to write about the economic system, but I believe his words can apply to the whole complex of reforms:

> One of the main reasons why we still do not have a proper basis for our economic reforms is that the government does not have a serious research center. . . . In my opinion we have a deep-rooted and false tradition embedded in our minds which lays it down that anybody occupying a high position has the right to rely only on his own intellect and to consider himself infallible.[22]

I do not know exactly whom Nazarbayev had in mind, but from what I have seen I share his opinion.

# Conclusion

When the great Russian poet Aleksandr Pushkin wrote a history of the peasant revolt led by Yemelyan Pugachev, he later commented, "At least I did my duty as an historian conscientiously: I sought diligently for the truth and set it down honestly, without trying to flatter either force or the fashionable way of thinking."[1] These words define the ideal for a historian.

Any historian has incomparably greater chances of making objective judgments when researching processes already complete than when examining current events. The biographer and the political scientist always have much greater opportunities to introduce into arguments and facts into their conclusions that have not yet been weighed in the scales of time. And this is often independent of a personal striving for the truth.

The book I have written is not a piece of historical research. In order to write a history of Perestroika it would be necessary to have many documents that are unavailable today, but even more so, events would have to retreat, so that they should not intrude into the mind of the contemporary researcher. Nevertheless the moral principles involved—the striving for objectivity and analysis, a refusal to submit to opportunism—were absolute for me. Someday we shall have a great many more facts and eyewitness accounts, from participants and leaders of the events. They may demand different answers, or even different questions, from mine. But I have written about Perestroika as I perceived it in its time, and I believe such a view will not be without interest for the future historian.

In our difficult times, so full of sudden explosions and so lacking in predictable developments, we continue to try to interpret Perestroika and the meaning of what was done and not done by its leader, Mikhail Gorbachev. Passions do not subside but get steadily more heated. And Perestroika and its originator continue as in previous years to be attacked from both the "right" and the "left."

The fact that the future is unknown reduces my compatriots to a state of confusion. Yes, I also believe and hope, as Gorbachev said in his last public speech as President, that "sooner or later our joint efforts will bear fruit. Our peoples will live in a prosperous and democratic society."[2] But confidence that things will turn out "sooner or later" does nothing to get rid of the problems arising from our ignorance of what will happen tomorrow.

We, my country and my people, can no longer be driven back into that dead end we have escaped. Only that is no guarantee that we shall not find ourselves in a different cul de sac. History does not shut the door on an advance to nowhere. The path will be chosen by our present-day politicians, who are pushed, more often than they would wish, by the logic of conflict and confrontation rather than good sense. What will the people, afraid for their own future, say to them? Will they say anything? Will they remain silent as happened so often in the past? Will they again display their patience to the point at which their voices will not be channeled by the democratic instruments of power but will have to ring out on the barricades thrown up by our latest social cataclysm?

Questions after questions.

As I reflect on the years that have passed, the judgments I have made and what I did myself, I want to say once again that I do not regret the choice I made in the Perestroika period. But I see the mistakes I made. I understand that in my position I did not do everything that was possible and necessary.

And if we are to discuss personal matters I would like to acquaint the reader with the signs which, according to Lev Tolstoy, determine what are for me the most important dates in those years. You will recall that I referred to his book *Thoughts of Wise Men for Everyday Use*, and a certain mysticism surrounding, "by the way of this book," two dates in the life of Mikhail Gorbachev?

Gorbachev was transferred from independent work in the Literary Institute to work in the Central Committee of the CPSU on July 20. On that day Tolstoy's book says, "He who says 'I love God' but hates his brother is a liar, because, not loving his brother whom he sees, how can he love God whom he does not see?" (The Epistle of St. John, IV, 20). And again: "Do justice to someone near to you — you can do it whether you love him or not — and you will learn to love him. But if you are unjust to him because you do not love him you will finish by hating him" (John Ruskin).

It is not for me to judge to what extent I succeeded in following these instructions. I am not a mystic, and it was only quite recently that I got to know these commandments. You can't live your life backwards.

Finally, here is what Tolstoy wrote on January 2, the date after which all the employees of the *apparat* of the President of the USSR were dismissed from their jobs because the presidential power structure had been abolished:

> People find it difficult, get worried and upset only when they are dealing with external affairs that do not depend on them. In such cases they ask themselves in some alarm: 'What am I going to do? What will happen? What will this produce? What if this or that happens?' That is how it is with people who are constantly concerned about what does not belong to them.
> On the other hand, a person who . . . devotes his life to the task of self-improvement will not be so inclined to worry. If he started to worry about whether he would succeed in keeping to the truth and avoiding the lie then

I would say: take it easy—what is worrying you is in your own hands—just watch your thoughts and your deeds.

The person who wants to succeed in worldly affairs gets no sleep night after night, keeps fussing and rushing about, ingratiates himself with powerful people, and behaves in general like a rogue. But in the end what has he got out of it? He has succeeded in being decorated with some honors, in being feared, and in having the power, so that he is a boss, to order people about. Surely you want to make the effort to free yourself from all these worries and to sleep peacefully, fearing nothing and being tormented by nothing? But such peace of mind is not easily achieved (Epictetus).[3]

There is profound truth in those words.

No honest person who has once plunged into the abyss of political activity or government service will assert that in such professions it is possible to perform noble tasks and not ignoble ones. Ideally, perhaps. But in this sinful world, in any service in which the fate of human beings depends on you, it is never possible to extract oneself from those contradictions.

I can say with confidence only this: what a good thing it is that I arrived at thoughts and judgments like these long before events drew a line under a whole epoch. It was a line that included my political career and my actions. I was rather late in drawing these conclusions for myself, but it came before the storm. My witnesses are the most exacting, my closest, and most trusted friends.

My life is ahead of me. And still ahead, I hope, is my scholarly and creative work. And God preserve me from ever agreeing to take up political work again.

There will always be politics. But let other people be involved in it—people who are made for it. I lived in that field, though for only a short time, and I saw what politics and politicians are like. For a historian and a political scientist that is an indispensable piece of luggage.

# Notes

*The quotations used in this book are translated from the Russian versions provided by Vladimir Yegorov, and the sources cited in the notes are primarily Russian editions. Where possible, an English title has been included for the reader's convenience.*

## Introduction
1. Vladislav Khodasevich. *Stikhotvoreniya* (Poems). Moscow, 1991, p. 81.
2. Vitali Zverev. *Grustny Put Vladislava Khodasevicha* (The Sad Career of Vladislav Khodasevich). Moscow, 1991, p. 13.

## 1   Designs in the Arras
1. Thornton Wilder. *The Eighth Day*, ed 1. New York, Evanston, London: Harper and Row, 1967, p. 435.
2. Ivan Ilyin. *Chto sulit miru raschlenleniye Rossii* (What Does the Breakup of Russia Mean for the World?). Quoted from *Literaturnaya Rossiya*, Moscow, 1991, p. 6.
3. Niccolo Machiavelli. *Gosudar* (The Prince). *Selected Works*. Moscow, 1982, pp. 349–350.
4. M. S. Gorbachev. *Perestroika i novoye myshleniye dlya nashei strany i dlya vsyego mira* (Perestroika: New Thinking for Our Country and the World). Moscow, 1987, pp. 11, 51.

5. Aleksandr Tsipko. "Boyus novogo Kerenskogo" (I Fear Another Kerensky). Interview in *Komsomolskaya Pravda*, March 16, 1991.
6. Aleksandr Yakovlev. "Democracy in Haste . . ." Interview in the *Literaturnaya Gazeta*, December 25, 1991.
7. Eduard Shevardnadze. *Moi bybor: V zashchitu demokratii i svobody* (My Choice). Moscow, 1991, p. 23.

## 2 Was Perestroika Really Necessary?

1. A. D. Sakharov. *Razmyshleniye o progresse, mirnom sosushchestvovanii i intellektualnoi svobode*. (Reflections on Progress, Peaceful Coexistence and Intellectual Freedom). "Trevoga i nadezhda" (Alarm and Hope). Moscow, 1990, pp. 28, 36–37.
2. M. S. Gorbachev. *Izbranniye rechi i stati* (Selected Speeches and Articles); vol. 4, p. 301.
3. Boris Yeltsin. *Ispoved na zadannuyu temu* (Confession on a Set Theme). Vilnius, 1990, pp. 54–55.
4. Yegor Ligachev. *V Kremle i na Staroi ploshchadi* (In The Kremlin and The Old Square). *Sovetskaya Rossiya*, no. 47, 1991.
5. Boris Yeltsin. Speech at 27th Congress of CPSU, February 26, 1986. *Rossiya segodnya: Politicheski portret v dokumentakh 1985–1991* (Russia Today: A Political Portrait in Documents 1985–1991). Moscow, 1991, p. 407.
6. Facts about pre-revolutionary Russia taken from B. Brazol, "The Reign of the Emperor Nicholas II 1894–1917," *The Russian Frontiers*, pp. 175, 177. Also I. I. Mints, *Istoria Velikogo Oktyabrya* (History of the Great October Revolution), vol. I. Moscow, 1967, pp. 40, 63, 99.
7. G. I. Khanin. *Dinamika ekonomicheskogo razvitiya CCCP* (The Dynamics of Economic Development of the USSR). Novosibirsk, 1991, p. 145.
8. L. A. Gordon, E.V. Klopov. *Chto eto bylo? Razmyshleniya o predposilkakh i itogakh togo chto sluchilos s nami v 30–40 gody* (What Was It? Thoughts Concerning the Prerequisites and Results of What Happened to Us in the 1930s and 1940s). Moscow, 1987, pp. 73–76, 162–163. Also V. P. Danilov. "Kollektivisatsiya selskogo khozyaistva v CCCP" (The Collectivization of Agriculture in the USSR); *The History of the USSR*, 1990, no. 5, p. 28.
9. G. I. Khanin, op. cit., p. 156.
10. See *Istoriya sotsialisticheskoi ekonomiki CCCP* (History of the Socialist Economy of the USSR). Moscow, 1980, vol. 7., p. 197. Also

E. Z. Maiminas. *Konteksty ekonomicheskoi reformy* (The Contexts of the Economic Reform). Moscow, 1989, p. 423. And G. I. Khanin, op. cit., p. 193.
11. See E. Z. Maiminas, op. cit., p. 425.

## 3 Why Gorbachev?

1. Quoted from S. A. Chibiryayev. *A Great Russian Reformer: The Life, Work and Political Views of M. M. Speransky*, Moscow, 1989, pp. 4, 89.
2. P. A. Stolypin. "We Need a Great Russia . . ." *Complete Collection of Speeches Delivered in the State Duma and State Council, 1906–1911*. Moscow, 1991, pp. 90, 96.
3. *Our Fatherland. An Essay in Political History*, vol. 2. Moscow, 1991, p. 555.
4. F. W. Kristians. *Roads to Russia*. Moscow, 1990, p. 138.
5. Yegor Ligachev, op. cit.
6. M. S. Gorbachev. *Selected Speeches and Articles,* vol. 5, p. 56.
7. See A. A. Gromyko. *Memoirs*, Book Two. Moscow, 1988, pp. 392–393. Also *Kommunist*, 1985, no. 5, pp. 6–7.
8. Aleksandr Tsipko, op. cit.
9. See Mikhail Heller. *The Seventh Secretary: The Rise and Fall of Mikhail Gorbachev*. London, 1991, pp. 25–30.

## 4 The Philosophy of Renewal

1. V. I. Lenin. *Complete Works*, vol. 45, p. 376.
2. N. A. Berdyaev. *The Origin and Meaning of Russian Communism*. Moscow, 1990, p. 102.
3. Georgi Fedotov. "The Fate of Our Intellectual Culture." *Dialog*, no. 18, 1991, pp. 42–43.
4. Erich Fromm. *Escape From Freedom*. Moscow, 1990, pp. 98, 227.
5. V. M. Mezhuev. "Socialism as an Idea and as a Reality." *Voprosy filosofii*, no. 11, 1991, p. 29.
6. M. S. Gorbachev. *Selected Speeches and Articles*; vol. 2, p. 154; *Izvestiya*, no. 202, August 24, 1991.
7. Ibid, vol. 4, p. 38.
8. Ibid, p. 87.
9. Ibid, p. 110.

10. Ibid, p. 425.
11. Ibid, vol. 5, p. 485.
12. Ibid, vol. 6, p. 342.

## 5   Gorbachev and Public History

1. V. O. Klyuchevsky. *Complete Works in Nine Volumes*, vol. VII, p. 382.
2. Stephen Cohen. "Perestroika—A Journey in Search of Something New . . ." *Kommunist*, no. 7, 1989, p. 24.
3. Valentin Rasputin. "Curses Get You Nowhere . . ." *Dialog*, no. 4, 1990, p. 107.
4. Robert Tucker. "What Time Is It by the Clock of Russian History?" *Dialog*, no. 4, 1991, p. 78.
5. Heller, op. cit., pp. 291–292.
6. *M. S. Gorbachev in the Sverdlovsk Region, 25–27 April 1990*. Moscow, 1990, p. 4.
7. See Vladmir Boikov. "Perestroika, Ideology and the Authority of the Party," *Dialog*, no. 4, Dialog, p. 3.
8. Ibid.
9. See N. Shipanov, I. Yakovento. "Ratings," *Dialog*, no. 10, 1990, p. 8.
10. *The Thoughts of Wise People for Everyday Use*, collected by Lev Tolstoy. Reprint of 1903 edition. Moscow, 1990, p. 378.
11. Ibid.
12. See "Historical Awareness in Modern Political Culture," *The Working Class and the Modern World*, no. 4, 1989, p. 93.
13. See *Historical Awareness: Its State and Tendency to Develop in Conditions of Perestroika*. Center for Sociological Research at the Academy of Social Science attached to the Central Committee of the CPSU. Information bulletin, no. 1 (10), 1991, p. 26.
14. Ibid, pp. 43, 53.

## 6   Evolution, Revolutionary Evolution, Revolution

1. F. M. Dostoevsky. *Complete Works in 30 Vols.*, vol. 21, p. 93.
2. K. Marx and Friedrich Engels. *Works*, vol. 36, p. 263.
3. S. I. Shidlovsky. "Reminiscences," *The Country Will Perish Today: The February Revolution of 1917*. Moscow, 1991, p. 147.
4. M. S. Gorbachev. *The August Coup: The Truth and the Lessons*. Moscow, 1991, pp. 70–71.

5. Marshall Goldman. *Gorbachev's Challenge: Economic Reform in the Age of Advanced Technology.* Moscow, 1988, pp. 253–254.
6. A. N. Yakovlev. "Hasty Democratization Will Not Produce . . ."
7. V. I. Zasulich, N. A. Dobrolyubov. *Rejected Writing, Book 1 (1900–1917).* Moscow, 1991, p. 125.
8. Richard Pipes. Interview with the magazine *Dialog*, no. 5, 1991, pp. 37–39.
9. Len Karpinsky. Article in *Moskovskiye Novosty*, no. 21, May 27, 1990.
10. Thomas Naylor. *Gorbachev's Strategy: The Opening of a Closed Society.* Moscow, 1988, p. 16.
11. Richard Pipes. Interview with *Dialog*, p. 42.
12. Boris Yeltsin. "Speech at the 4th Congress of People's Deputies of the USSR," *Russia Today: A Political Portrait with Documents, 1985–1991.* Moscow, 1991, p. 487.
13. M. S. Gorbachev. *The August Coup*, p. 45.
14. G. V. Plekhanov. *Works*, vol. 12, p. 66.

# 7  What Happened in the Perestroika Years?

1. V. V. Rozanov, *Works*, vol. 1. Moscow, 1990, p. 161.
2. Quoted from B. L. Gubman, *The Sense of History: Studies in Modern Western Ideas.* Moscow, 1991, p. 36.
3. A. I. Solzhenitsyn. "How We Can Reorganize Russia: Tentative Ideas," *Komsomolskaya Pravda*, special edition. Moscow, 1990, p. 9.
4. Aleksandr Zinovyev. "I Want to Tell You About the West," *Mind the Fatal Line.* Moscow, 1991, p. 217.
5. T. I. Zaslavskaya. *Perestroika and Socialism.* Moscow, 1989, p. 217.
6. *Russia Today: A Political Picture in Documents*, p. 307.
7. M. S. Gorbachev. *The August Coup*, pp. 67–68.
8. See Marshall Goldman, op. cit., pp. 94, 95.
9. E. Maiminas. "Can an Economic System Be Just?" *Free Thought*, no. 16, 1991.
10. See Vladimir Boikov. "The Market: A Majority in Favor." *Dialog*, no. 8, 1991, p. 3.
11. See T. Zaslavskaya. *The Strategy of the Social Control of Perestroika: There Is No Other Way.* Moscow, 1988, pp. 11, 25.

12. See S. Lebedev, I. Yakovenko. "Ratings," *Dialog*, no. 11, 1990, p. 3.
13. See T. I. Zaslavskaya. "Socialism, Perestroika and Public Opinion." *Sociological Studies*, no. 8, 1991, pp. 14, 15.
14. Ibid.
15. See L. A. Gordon. "The Working-Class Movement in a Post-Socialist Perspective." *Socialist Studies*, no. 8, 1991. pp. 14, 15.
16. Walter Laqueur. *The Long Road to Freedom: Russia and Glasnost*. Moscow, 1990, p. 294.
17. *Our Fatherland: An Essay in Political History*. Vol. 2, p. 610–611.
18. Heller, op. cit., pp. 413–414.
19. Thomas Naylor, *Gorbachev's Strategy: Opening Up a Closed Society*, p. 239.
20. Gorbachev, *The August Coup*, p. 5.
21. Ibid, p. 6.
22. Ibid, pp. 73, 75.
23. See S. Ustimenko. "The Crisis," *Dialog*, no. 11, 1991, p. 9.
24. A. Avtorkhanov. *The Empire of the Kremlin: The Soviet Type of Colonialism*. Vilnius, 1990, p. 216.
25. Gorbachev, *The August Coup*, pp. 78–80.
26. Ibid, pp. 33, 48.
28. See *The Population of the USSR*, results of a nationwide census of the population in 1979. Moscow, 1980, pp. 27–30.
29. See V. Boikov, "The Union Treaty," *Dialog*, no. 1, 1991, p. 47.
30. See Aleksandr Yakovlev, *Perestroika: Hopes and Realities*.
31. See A. D. Sakharov, *Alarm and Hope*, pp. 259, 264–265, 269–272.
32. Mikhail Heller, op. cit., p. 373.
33. Anatoli Sobchak. *The Way To Power*; second, revised edition. Moscow, 1991, p. 270.
34. Eduard Shevardnadze. *My Choice*, pp. 124–125.
35. A. Avtorkhanov, op. cit., pp. 230–231.
36. Raisa Gorbachev. "I Hope . . ." Moscow, 1991, p. 158.
37. Eduard Shevardnadze. *My Choice*, pp. 122, 128.

# 8  Gorbachev's Algorithm

1. Francis Bacon. *Novum Organum*, vol. 2. Moscow, 1972. p. 468.

2. G. F. Hegel. *Works*, vol. 8, pp. 25, 32.
3. J. W. Goethe. *Selected Philosophical Works*. Moscow, 1964, p. 377.
4. D. S. Merezhkovsky. *In A Quiet Pond: Articles and Studies*. Moscow, 1991, p. 467.
5. Antonio Rubbi. *Meetings with Gorbachev*. Moscow, 1991, pp. 20–21.
6. M. S. Gorbachev. *The August Coup*, pp. 89–90.
7. A. Yakovlev, op. cit., p. 166.
8. Yeltsin, *Confession on a Set Theme*, p. 91.
9. Yegor Ligachev. *The Gorbachev Riddle*, 1991, p. 48.
10. T. Zaslavskaya. *The Strategy of the Social Control of Perestroika*, pp. 38–40.
11. Ibid, pp. 40–41.
12. Vladimir Vyunitsky. "Algorithm," *Dialog*, no. 4, 1991, p. 46.
13. From Yeltsin's speech on central television on February 19, 1991. *Komsomolskaya Pravda*, February 22, 1991.
14. A. E. Presnyakov. *Russian Autocrats*. Moscow, 1990, pp. 137–138.
15. G. F. Hegel. *The Philosophy of Law*. Moscow, 1990, p. 354.
16. Vladimir Vyunitsky, op. cit., pp. 46–47.
17. Gorbachev, *The August Coup*, p. 66.
18. Quoted by Boris Litvak, "Aleksandr Romanov, Mikhail Gorbachev," *Top Secret*, no. 10, 1991, p. 2.
19. "Gorbachev Prepared the Committee for the Emergency." Statement by Oleg Shenin to the Russian Prosecutor, no. 4, 1991.
20. See Eduard Shevardnadze, *My Choice*, p. 342.
21. A. Butenko. "What is Happening to Us?" *Kultura*, no. 8, 1991.
22. Nursultan Nazarbayev. *Without Rights or Lefts*. Moscow, 1991, pp. 186–187, 201–202.

## Conclusion

1. A. S. Pushkin. *Complete Works in Ten Volumes*, vol. 10. Leningrad, 1979, p. 510.
2. M. S. Gorbachev, "I Believe in Our Wisdom . . ." *Sovetskaya Rossiya*, December 27, 1991.
3. Tolstoy, op. cit., p. 188.

# Vladimir K. Yegorov

Being named chancellor of the Soviet Union's Institute of Literature in 1985 meant more to Vladimir K. Yegorov than simply reaching the pinnacle of a dedicated academic career.

For this philosopher, historian, and man of letters, the moment presented a dramatic opportunity to observe, from the inside, the government of a social system that had been the focus of his studies and fascination for almost twenty years.

While it was among Mikhail Gorbachev's first official acts as the newly elected General Secretary of the Communist Party's Central Committee, confirming Yegorov's appointment must have seemed incidental to this man who knew his country needed fundamental change to survive.

Yet, in history's hindsight, the appointment was neither incidental nor simply the peculiar laboratory of a social scholar. Yegorov was to become one of Gorbachev's closest advisors and, if not an architect of Perestroika, a master craftsman whose work was to give life and reality to those policies.

Born in 1947 into a family of teachers and descendants of farmers in the small, provincial town of Kanasch, Yegorov's is a story of rags to riches, at least in the context of the Soviet Union. His mother Elisabeth, a teacher of Russian language and literature at the nearby teachers college, raised him and his sister alone after his family separated in 1950.

In a sense, she had been well prepared for this. The eldest of seven children, Elisabeth became responsible for her sibling's welfare and upbringing when her father, a priest, disappeared during the oppression of the Stalinist era.

Despite the hardships, or perhaps because of them, Elisabeth instilled in her children a strong appreciation for education and intellectual curiosity. Vladimir was an excellent student in high school and went on to study history and philosophy on full scholarships at the University of Kasan. Kasan is Russia's most prestigious university and the institution where Leo Tolstoy and Vladimir Ilyich Lenin received their educations.

After concluding his undergraduate studies in 1971, Yegorov stayed on to earn his doctorate in 1974, choosing as his thesis, "The Participation of the Farmers in the October Revolution in 1917."

As a young teacher, Yegorov became a lector to the Central Committee's youth organization, KOMSOMOL, in Moscow. KOMSOMOL, by law, was the leadership reservoir of the Communist Party of the Soviet Union. He completed his work there as head of the Department of Propaganda, and then became Deputy Editor in Chief of the idealogical magazine, *The Young Communist*, an official publication with a circulation of 300,000.

Writers and editors for *The Young Communist* increasingly were of the younger communist generation and, as a consequence, many were heavily influenced by the spirit of the Krushchev era. As an early sign of dissent at the beginning of the 1980s, many of these writers and editors, including Yegorov, began moving to, or contributing articles to, the magazine, *Literaturnaya Gazeta*. At that time, the *Gazeta* was the only public voice for members of the intellectual circles of the Soviet Union.

Yegorov was in a rather unique position; he enjoyed the trust and respect of both the intellectuals among the oppositionists and the moderates within the party. Indeed, just before his appointment to the Institute of Literature, he headed the international communications center of the World Youth and Student Festival in Moscow.

The advent of Perestroika attracted the support of members of the scientific and artistic community, and Yegorov was their unofficial liaison with the party.

Two years after his appointment as chancellor, he was summoned to Perestroika headquarters and made Deputy Secretary of the Cultural Department. Following the reorganization of the Central Committee, he was named Deputy Secretary of the Department of Ideology and Under Secretary for Cultural Affairs.

It was in his capacity in these later positions that Mikhail Gorbachev tapped Yegorov to be one of his advisors. Yegorov had reached the inner circle, responsible for cultural affairs, religious organizations and was now a much more official liaison to the intellectual community. He remained in that position until Gorbachev's resignation in December 1991, and in January 1992 became a member of the Academy of Science of Russia in Moscow, the analytical center of social-economic and science-technological affairs. He has written many articles for *Literaturnaya Gazeta* on latter-day Soviet culture and the ramifications of the tremendous sociological changes that have occurred there.

Yegorov, who is married and has a teen-aged son, lives in Moscow and has written a number of books, including *History is the Change of Generations, History in Our Life,* and *A Star is Fading.* However, his chronicle of his life inside the Gorbachev government and his scholarly analysis of Perestroika were reserved for his latest book, *Out of a Dead End, Into the Unknown.*